STUDIES IN THE BRITISH ECONOMY

PRICING IN PRACTICE

D1794728

STUDIES IN THE BRITISH ECONOMY

General Editor: Derek Lee

Core Book: The United Kingdom Economy *by NIESR*
Monopoly *by C. Pass and J. Sparkes*
Regional Planning and the Location of Industry *by D. Lee*
Britain's Overseas Trade *by V. Anthony*
Government Intervention and Industrial Policy *by A. Skuse*
The Trade Unions *by H. Williamson*
Control of the Economy *by D. Lee*
Banks and Markets *by V. Anthony*
National Economic Planning *by C. Sandford*
National Income and Expenditure *by S. Hays*
The Structure of British Industry *by M. Dunn and P. Tranter*
The Engineering Industries *by S. Hays*
The Distributive Trades *by F. Livesey*
British Population *by R. M. Williams*
The Chemical and Allied Industries *by S. Hays*
The United Kingdom and the World Monetary System
  by B. Davies
Britain, the EEC and the Developing World *by M. McQueen*
Pricing in Practice *by J. Davies and S. Hughes*
Business Finance and the City of London *by Brinley Davies*
Britain and the European Economic Community *by D. Lewis*
Britain's Agricultural Industry *by B. Hill*
Trade and Growth *by C. Pass and J. Sparkes*
Investment in British Industry *by J. R. Davies and S. Hughes*

STUDIES IN THE BRITISH ECONOMY

Pricing in Practice

by
J. R. Davies
Senior Lecturer, North Staffordshire Polytechnic

and

S. Hughes
Senior Lecturer, Lanchester Polytechnic

HEINEMANN EDUCATIONAL BOOKS
LONDON

Heinemann Educational Books Ltd
22 Bedford Square, London WC1B 3HH

LONDON EDINBURGH MELBOURNE AUCKLAND
HONG KONG SINGAPORE KUALA LUMPUR NEW DELHI
IBADAN NAIROBI JOHANNESBURG
EXETER (NH) KINGSTON PORT OF SPAIN

ISBN 0 435 84563 2

Reproduced, printed and bound in Great Britain by
Fakenham Press Limited, Fakenham, Norfolk

CONTENTS

PREFACE

Most economics text books attempt to cover the subject within a single volume and in consequence some topics are treated briefly: often these same topics are those whose subject matter changes most rapidly. At present in order to keep up to date in the field of economics recourse must be made to a vast field of diffused literature including bank reviews, government publications, newspapers and various journals. With these problems in mind this series was conceived. The series consists of specialized books on those topics which are subject to frequent change or where the sources of information are too scattered to be readily available to the average student. It is intended that each book will be revised at frequent intervals in order to take account of new developments.

Derek Lee.

INTRODUCTION

Pricing has always been an interesting and important topic of economics. The subject of pricing, however, has become even more recently important with (a) entry by the U.K. into the Common Market and the increase in international competition; (b) the increasing role played by the public sector in the British economy; (c) the high rate of inflation that has existed in recent years.

The object of this work has been to give the student a broader understanding of pricing than is normally obtained from an 'A' level or first and second-year Polytechnic/University course in economic theory. The student who leaves school after 'A' Level may find his economic theory inadequate to understand the problem of determining prices, and for those who continue to Polytechnic/University, a further two years' study without an adequate introduction to business reality can lead to a too narrow and simplified approach to economic problems. We hope this work will fill that void and provide the student with an insight into the wider problems of pricing.

Chapter 1 discusses the controversy surrounding the question of whether or not profit maximization represents an accurate definition of business goals. It is only by understanding the objectives of a firm that one can appreciate the decisions they take and the prices they charge.

In Chapter 2 the role of prices in the economy in the allocation of scarce resources is discussed, and a Command Economy of the Soviet type is compared with a system which allows the free play of market forces.

Chapters 3, 5 and 6 look at the many factors that need to be taken into consideration for a firm operating in the private sector, such as costs, competition, product life-cycle etc., while Chapter 7 discusses the special problems of pricing in the nationalized industries.

Finally, in Chapter 8 we conclude by discussing the role of the government in influencing prices.

1 BUSINESS OBJECTIVES

1. Introduction

Most of the literature concerned with business objectives has focused upon the controversy surrounding the question of whether or not 'profit maximization' is an adequate representation of business goals. Profit maximization is the objective assumed in the traditional economic theory of the firm. However, the traditional theory and the assumption of profit maximization in general has been subject to much criticism. This criticism has been centred partly on the divorce of ownership and control and the subsequent pursuit of other objectives; partly around the inherently uncertain nature of the business world and the resulting difficulties involved in achieving profit maximization; and partly on the fact that the firm of the traditional theory in no way resembles the business organizations of the real world. It is our purpose in this chapter to summarize and comment upon the main arguments in these controversies.

THE CONVENTIONAL THEORY OF THE FIRM

2. The entrepreneur and profit maximization

The traditional theory of the firm asserts that the decision-making of a firm is undertaken by an 'entrepreneur' whose actions are guided by the desire to maximize profits. It is this entrepreneur who brings together the other factors of production – land, labour and capital – and organizes them in a manner conducive to the efficient production of the goods and services demanded by the consuming public. Most important, it is the entrepreneur who takes the risk, for if the business fails then his reward may even be negative. Whereas the other factors of production know what payment they are going to receive for their services, the reward of the entrepreneur has no such certainty since it depends upon the success of his business. It is profit which is the reward of the entrepreneur and hence his desire to maximize profits.

3. Profits and the allocation of resources

Moreover, according to the traditional theory, it is the profit motive which leads to the efficient allocation of resources. If consumers demand more of a particular product, the increase in demand will push its price up, which in turn will lead to an increase in profits. This increase will persuade the entrepreneur to produce more of that good and will induce more entrepreneurs to enter the industry, thus increasing the output of the good. Moreover, the excess profits the entrepreneur is receiving will enable him to obtain more of the other factors of production because he will be able to pay them more than they could earn in industries where demand is declining. Thus it is through changes in the levels of profits that resources are reallocated the way consumers desire. Hence it is argued that profit maximization is a necessary though not sufficient condition for the efficient allocation of resources by the price system.

THE ATTACK ON PROFIT MAXIMIZATION

4. The divorce of ownership and control

The major criticism of the profit maximizing assumption has been the recognition that there is a very large area of business activity in which there is no longer a single entrepreneur who takes all the risks, makes all the major decisions, and takes all the profits. On the contrary, the owners – the shareholders – are no longer always in direct control of the business and the decision-takers may therefore be free to pursue objectives other than profit maximization. In addition, in large companies where the divorce of ownership and control is most pronounced, the executive management often see themselves as arbiters between the claims on the corporation.

5. The managerial revolution

The idea that the control of a company does not reside with the shareholders is not a new one. In 1940 James Burnham wrote of the *Managerial Revolution*.[1] Burnham pointed out that the wielding of economic power was not undertaken by the wealthiest men, that the growth of the large company had been accompanied by a divorce of ownership and control, and that control had fallen into the hands of a new class of managers whose ambitions were characterized by a craving for power rather than by the desire to generate wealth. It is probably true to say that the process was more of an evolution rather than a revolution, but the main points of Burnham's observations remain unquestionably accurate.

6. Structure of the company: shareholders versus directors

Theoretically the modern company is a democratic organization, its constituents being the holders of voting shares. The government of the company resides in the Annual General Meeting of the shareholders, and the board of directors as stipulated in the Articles of Association. In theory the general meeting has the power to appoint and remove directors, to make changes or to reject proposed changes in the Articles of Association, and also to appoint independent auditors to inspect the accounts. Thus, in theory, the control of the company resides with the shareholders.

In practice, however, these powers are largely illusory. In theory the shareholders choose the board of directors but in practice the board of directors often chooses itself. The shareholders merely confirm the appointed nominees of the directors. Similarly, proposed changes in the articles of association are initiated by the board of directors itself, though shareholders have the right to call a general meeting and initiate action provided more than 5 per cent of the voting strength agree.

However, the main weakness of the shareholders lies in their own nature and character. Florence[2] has estimated that 50 per cent of the largest British companies, and about 30 per cent of the next largest size, had no single controlling group of shareholders by the 1950s. The largest companies have hundreds of thousands of shareholders and consequently there is an absentee rate of over 99 per cent at most Annual General Meetings. Moreover, by their very nature, the small shareholders will want to spread their holdings among various companies in order to cut down the risk involved. It is this fragmentation of shareholdings which has delivered the crucial blow to shareholder control. Because their holdings are dispersed among various companies, the shareholders have insufficient time to attend the general meetings of all these companies. Moreover, shares are frequently held by children and many others not interested in the affairs of a particular company so long as they receive a regular return on their investment. The 1965 survey[3] by the London Stock Exchange demonstrated that the proportions of male and female shareholders were 60 per cent and 40 per cent respectively. It is for all these reasons that the theoretical power of the shareholders has in practice passed to the board of directors.

7. Structure of the company: directors versus management

Thus it would appear from the above that control lies with the self-appointed delegates of the shareholders – namely the board of directors. The function of the board of directors is to act as a link between the management and the shareholders, and to exercise a general supervision of policy. In large companies the board of directors meets intermittently and does not deal with day to day problems. It orders continuation or change in the direction of the business from time to time. The chief functions of the directors are the selection of executive officers, policy making, and the general supervision of performance. These functions would appear to be the top governing functions in the organization. In practice, however, just as the power of the board of directors itself has grown because of the inability of the shareholders meeting to govern a large company, so also the power of managing directors has grown because it is impossible for boards to determine all aspects of policy.

It was once thought that the board determined policy and the managers executed it. Legally this may still be possible since in Britain a company need not appoint a managing director, and even if an appointment is made his power may be defined so as to make him subservient to the board. However, in practice, the executives come to dominate the board meetings, and for two reasons. The first lies in the weakness of the directors themselves, some of whom are not technically familiar with the workings of the company. The age and character of non-executive directors, many of whom are appointed more for their reputation for honour rather than efficiency, works towards this end. However, more important is the second reason which lies in the strength of the managers themselves. Their strength arises from their superior technical efficiency and their earning power. Marris[4] points out that the earning capacity of the company does not reside in its physical assets but in the ability of the management team; that their ability to flatten the U shaped cost curve rendered them great bargaining power with which they are able to dominate board meetings. Similarly, Gilbert wrote 'The Board has become more and more a legal fiction in practice . . . and in many cases has been deposed by operating management.'[5] Thus it would appear that in practice it is the managers who are the real decision takers in industry.

8. Managerial motivation

The divorce of ownership and control has significant implications for the traditional theory of the firm. It is suggested that managers have objectives of their own and that they will actively pursue these objectives rather than pursue profit maximization. This argument becomes particularly strong once one begins to move away from perfectly competitive market structures, since profit maximization no longer becomes a total condition of survival. Burnham implied this when he suggested that it was the craving for power rather than the maximizing of profits that was the driving force behind the modern company executive.[6] It has been suggested that managerial salary tends to be linked to sales volume, and that consequently managers will attempt to maximize sales revenue or growth rather than profits. Baumol[7] has developed a sales revenue-maximizing theory of the firm while Marris has developed a growth-maximizing theory of the firm. O. E. Williamson[8] has developed a managerial discretion model of the firm in which he postulates a managerial utility function composed of such items as expenditure on executive staff, managerial slack (perks, etc.), and discretionary investment spending power. Williamson suggests that managers get positive utility from each of these variables, and will attempt to maximize the function. In contrast to the above models, Simon[9] has argued that the firm does not attempt to maximize anything, but is more concerned with satisficing, i.e. instead of being concerned with obtaining the maximum possible return the company is contented with a return which it regards as being reasonable. Similarly, Scitovsky[10] argues that leisure is also part of the managerial utility function, and that managers aim at some kind of trade-off between leisure and income. More recently, Leibenstein[11] with his concept of X-inefficiency has suggested that in large organizations managers and workers alike are settling for the quiet life rather than become engaged in the competitive pressures which profit maximization entails.

9. The responsible corporation

Another line of argument is that companies are increasingly beginning to realize their responsible role in society. Director responsibilities, according to the Institute of Directors, extend to the company, its shareholders, employees, customers and creditors, and also to the state. There is now a widely held view that the fundamental test of any business is whether it serves society well; in particular, whether it provides good values to customers, good, well-paid jobs to its employees, and a reasonable rate of return to its owners.

The legal position is that the law still requires directors to act in the interests of the shareholders alone, and that the interests of employees, customers, etc., should be taken account of only in so far as they coincide with the interests of the shareholders. In practice, however, a company depends upon the goodwill of employees, customers and the community, and the directors could justify almost any measure on behalf of any one of these groups as being an act of goodwill and consequently in the interests of the shareholders.

10. The behavioural theory – the concept of organizational goals

Cyert and March[12] have taken a completely different approach from most other theories of the firm and challenged the idea of a single entrepreneurial decision-taking unit which has a single-minded objective of its own. They argue that organizations themselves do not have goals, and that it is only the individual members of the organizations that can have goals. Moreover, they argue that the organization is composed of many elements (shareholders, workers, management, customers, etc.) each of which have goals of their own. They see the firm as a coalition in which goal-conflicts among the participants are never permanently resolved. The effective goals of the firm in any given situation are governed by the bargaining process which fixes the composition of the coalition. Side payments are made to members of the organization in order to obtain conformity to the goals that arise from this bargaining process. These side payments may be in the form of money, personal treatment, authority or organizational policy. The result is that various goals arise from this bargaining process which may in themselves be conflicting, but which may still be viable in that they will be attended to at different points in time. The consequence of this process is that the firm will be seeking a satisfactory level of performance so that instead of maximizing in one utility dimension such as profits, it will be satisficing in a number of utility dimensions.

11. The effect of uncertainty

One of the earliest criticisms of the traditional theory of the firm was that profit maximization depended upon knowledge of demand and cost functions and the equation of marginal revenue and marginal cost functions of which, on the whole, businessmen had very little knowledge. Thus, it was argued that businessmen engaged in full-cost pricing rather than in the marginalism required for profit maximization. However, it can be argued that the variation in the profit margin in the full-cost pricing approach is tantamount to profit maximization (see Chapter 5).

A second effect of uncertainty is on the managerial models of the firm. Since the managerial rewards of risk-taking are low in relation to the managerial risk of failure (replacement), managers will tend to pursue a 'safety first' policy which will not be conducive to profit maximization. However, a more generous use of stock option schemes and share bonuses may help to redress this balance.

The behavioural model argues that the firm reacts to uncertainty by employing standardized decision rules that emphasize reaction to short-run feedback, rather than pursuit of long-run strategies.

12. Profit as a constraint

Perhaps the most significant feature of all these theories of the firm is that they contain profit as an element. The crucial question is whether profit is an objective in its own right or merely a constraint which has to be satisfied in order to achieve other objectives. Baumol[13] and Marris[14] have developed models using profit as a constraint, suggesting that a certain amount of profit has to be earned to keep the shareholders satisfied and that once this level of profit has been attained the managers are free to pursue their own objectives.

REINSTATEMENT OF PROFIT AS AN OBJECTIVE

13. The market structure argument

The market structure in the industries where the divorce of owner-ship and control is most pronounced tends to make the share-holder objective coincide with the objectives of the managers. The oligopolistic market structure which tends to characterize these industries means that a firm's relative strength and hence bargaining power depends on such things as market share, relative size, etc. Thus, according to Rothschild[15] the safety motive then becomes as important as the profit motive. One could equally well contend, however, that in an oligopolistic industry the profit objective is achieved via the safety motive; i.e. that in an oligopolistic industry safety becomes synonymous with profit. If one accepts this, it is not difficult to see that the managerial objectives of maximizing sales, growth, etc., and responsible corporation objectives of paternally wooing the customers, employees and society, all represent part of the firm's roundabout way of pursuing the profit motive and, as such, coincide with the objectives of the shareholders.

14. The special role of profits

Profits maximization is of supreme importance because it enables the attainment of all other goals, i.e. lower prices, higher wages, better quality, etc. A point worth noting is that profitability and rate of return on capital is becoming the nationalized industries' most useful working criterion.

15. Increased shareholder power

Shareholders have more influence than is sometimes suggested. The Companies Act of 1948 and 1967 took steps to prevent shareholder exploitation. Shareholders' rights were increased by enabling dissatisfied shareholders to use the company machinery to raise opposition to company policy, and also by increasing the power of the Board of Trade to intervene on their behalf, but the most notable change was the inclusion in the Companies Act of 1967 of the requirement that all limited companies file their annual accounts with the Registrar of Companies, thus giving shareholders far more financial information about the companies they owned.

A survey conducted for the London Stock Exchange in 1965 demonstrated that 93 per cent of the adult population in Great Britain had money saved or invested in one form or another.[16] However, only 7 per cent were themselves shareholders (and this included those holding unit and investment trusts), the remainder investing indirectly through the various institutional channels, with insurance policies alone accounting for 63 per cent of the indirect investors.

Similarly a survey of Fisons' shareholders in 1969 demonstrated that institutions held 45 per cent of the Fisons' shares, and this was judged to be fairly typical. This survey also showed that institutional investors tend to be committed to long-term holdings. The responsibilities which institutional management carries on behalf of its investors and the difficulty of disposing of large blocks of shares could mean that the institutions will play an increasing part in company affairs in the future.[17]

16. The capital market constraint

The shareholders ultimate weapon of control, however, lies not in the post-war company legislation, but in their ability to sell their shares if they are dissatisfied and in the ease with which shares can be sold on the Stock Exchange.

It is sometimes argued that for large companies the capital market constraint becomes inoperative since they can raise their financial requirements internally. However, if a firm is concerned with sales and growth objectives, then it is unlikely to limit itself to internal finance. Moreover, it is precisely when managers are pursuing expansionary objectives that the shareholders' ultimate weapon becomes all powerful. For if the company is successfully to raise additional finance from the market, then it must be in a position where its share prices and dividend distribution are attractive. Hence, shareholder objectives cannot be ignored.

17. Conclusion

In conclusion, it may be said that profit maximization is not pursued all the time by all firms. Nevertheless, profit is important in all firms even if it merely enters as a constraint. To admit that businesses do not always strictly adhere to a policy of profit maximization is not to invalidate its use as one criterion. Certainly no other more complete criterion has yet been suggested.

REFERENCES

1. James Burnham, *The Managerial Revolution*, Penguin Books, reprinted 1962.
2. P. S. Florence, *Ownership, Control and Success in Large Companies*, Sweet and Maxwell, 1961.
3. 'How Does Britain Save?', Survey by the London Stock Exchange, 1966.
4. R. Marris, *The Economic Theory of Managerial Capitalism*, Macmillan, 1964.
5. L. D. and J. J. Gilbert, *Report of Stockholder Activities during 1958*, New York, 1959.
6. Burnham, op. cit.
7. W. J. Baumol, *Business Behaviour, Value and Growth*, Harcourt, Brace and World, 1966.
8. O. E. Williamson, *The Economics of Discretionary Behaviour: Managerial Objectives in a theory of the firm*, Prentice-Hall, 1964.
9. H. A. Simon, *New Developments in the Theory of the Firm, A.E.R.*, May 1962.
10. T. Scitovsky, *Welfare and Competition*, Allen & Unwin, revised edition 1971.
11. H. Leibenstein, 'Allocative Efficiency versus X-Efficiency', *A.E.R.*, June 1966.
12. R. M. Cyert and J. G. March, *A Behavioural Theory of the Firm*, Prentice-Hall, 1963.
13. Baumol, op. cit.
14. Marris, op. cit.
15. K. W. Rothschild, 'Price Theory and Oligopoly', *E.J.*, 1947.
16. London Stock Exchange Survey, op. cit.
17. See Chapter 11 by H. Redwood in *Handbook of Strategic Planning*, edited by B. Taylor and K. Hawkins, Longmans, 1971.

PROGRESS TEST

(Numbers in brackets refer to paragraph numbers in the chapter)

1. Explain the function of the entrepreneur and suggest why he is likely to be a profit maximizer. (2)

2. Why are profits so important to the operation of the price mechanism? (3)
3. What criticisms have been made of the traditional theory of the firm? (1, 4, 5, 8, 9, 10, 11)
4. To what extent is there a divorce of ownership and control in British industry? (4, 5, 6, 7, 8)
5. Explain the term 'Managerial Revolution'. (5)
6. What are the alternative theories of the firm? (8, 9, 10)
7. Explain the term 'Organizational Goals'. (10)
8. What arguments can you use to support the profits maximization assumption? (2, 3, 13, 14, 15, 16, 17)

2 THE ROLE OF PRICES IN THE ECONOMY

THE FREE PLAY OF MARKET FORCES

1. Introduction

When the early economists began studying the economy what fascinated them more than anything else was the way in which a national economy could be run and co-ordinated without any apparent outside interference or any one person or group of persons planning the whole operation. If the successful operation of one firm involves the concentrated effort of some of the best business brains, and even then success is not guaranteed, what factor was controlling and co-ordinating the entire economy? Adam Smith[1] spoke of the 'invisible hand' of the price mechanism as guiding and controlling the economy, and classical theory was based on this belief – that market forces could co-ordinate economic activity and lead to an allocation of scarce resources which would enable a nation to obtain the maximum benefit.

2. The price mechanism

The theory of demand explains how a consumer distributes his income between various commodities, price and utility determining the quantity he will purchase of each good or service. His demand for a product and the price he will be prepared to pay will act as a signal mechanism for the producers, who, knowing their costs of production, can determine profitability and move in response to that signal. They in turn demand factors of production and to attract them they might have to increase the price previously offered.

The consumer's willingness to pay tells the entrepreneur he wants more or less of a product, and motivated by profit the entrepreneur will react to these responses and thus the effective allocation of resources in the economy is achieved.

Excessive waste of resources will be avoided because the consumers will only be prepared to pay a small price, if any price at all, for a product which gives them little utility. This makes the production of that product unprofitable and therefore resources will be diverted from producing that product to producing something which the consumer has indicated (through offering a high price) that he wants.

3. Optimum allocation of resources

The optimum allocation of resources is achieved because the whole operation takes place in the hypothetical world of perfect competition.

Under these conditions prices will tend to equality with marginal cost (MC) and every producer will operate at his point of minimum average cost (AC).

This means that:

(a) Every firm is operating at peak efficiency at the lowest point on its AC curves.

(b) Productive resources are distributed between commodities in exactly the right pattern.

(c) Each firm earns only 'normal' profits. Price therefore is influenced by demand and in turn influences the level of profits to be earned in different sectors of the total market. Entrepreneurs motivated by the desire to maximize profits will move resources into sectors where profits exceed the 'normal' level and move resources out of sectors where profits are below the 'normal' level.

4. An ideal which does not exist

The mechanism we have described above is an ideal which in practice does not exist. The operation of the mechanism assumes many simplifications which, when introduced in reality, can lead to an allocation of resources which can be far from the ideal envisaged.

We shall now list the assumptions on which the above mechanism is based, then take each assumption in turn and compare it with what is the case in reality.

The efficient operation of the price mechanism assumes:

(a) Consumers act rationally.

(b) Perfect competition.

(c) Factors of production are mobile.
(d) Equal distribution of income.
(e) No public or national goods.
(f) No divergence between private and social cost and benefits.

5. Consumers act rationally

For consumers to act rationally they must be acting with knowledge of all the choices open to them and with knowledge of the merits and de-merits of the various products and services which they are being offered. Yet in 1973 the circulation of the consumer-guidance magazine *Which* was only 650,000.[2] Only a tiny proportion of families, mainly drawn from the middle-classes, make use of this sort of detailed factual consumer information.

The consumers are, moreover, being subjected to a barrage of advertisements, very few providing information and for the most part extolling other reasons why consumers should purchase the product, which have very little to do with the product itself. With items that are subject to repeat purchase this problem is not too great. Over 60 per cent of consumers' expenditure is on such products where experimentation is easy and not damaging,[3] since the consumer can refuse to repurchase an unsatisfactory product. However, for consumer durables where the initial layout is large and purchases infrequent, mistaken purchase through poor information can be very harmful to the consumer.

We must be careful, however, not to exaggerate the influence of advertising. At one time 90 per cent of all new products were failures that eventually had to be withdrawn from the market. Some recent figures suggest that this percentage is now only 80 per cent, an improvement still alarmingly high for producers.

There are numerous examples that demonstrate that advertising expenditure cannot do everything; for example in September 1957 Ford's launched the *Edsel*, a medium priced car. Production was discontinued after only two years for despite intensive advertising, sales fell from 54,500 in the last quarter of 1957 to 26,500 and 29,500 in the years 1958 and 1959 respectively. Another example is when Lever Brothers introduced in the early 1960s a toilet soap, *Lyril*, accompanied by an advertising campaign costing £1m. During the first few months it gained some 8/9 per cent of the toilet soap market; thereafter sales began to decline and it was subsequently withdrawn.

The above examples have been given so that we can look at the problem in perspective. We must be careful not to credit advertising with too much influence; yet it has created the atmosphere of mass consumption and conspicuous consumption which have no doubt undermined consumer sovereignty to some extent.[4]

Consumer sovereignty implies choice, yet the range of options open to the consumer is largely determined by the producer and in many cases this can mean either merely a choice of label or frivolous and wasteful forms of differentiation. The trends in section 6 below are working to undermine consumer sovereignty. 'The extreme view that consumer sovereignty has been totally usurped is exaggerated. But certainly there has been a major shift to producer power since economists first elaborated their theory of the market in which the consumer always held the initiative.'[5]

6. Perfect competition

In most markets some degree of monopoly exists and our economy is becoming more and more oligopolistic. This means that no longer will we have an equilibrium where price is equal to MC and every producer is producing at the minimum point on his AC curve.

Chapter 1 indicated that with the divorce of ownership and control firms pursued motives other than the maximization of profit and this means that firms are no longer likely to move in response to consumer demand in such a way as always to guarantee an optimum allocation of resources. The existence of barriers to entry also means that firms are prevented from moving into areas where profits exceed 'normal' and demand exceeds supply. In Britain the largest 100 firms account for over half of all profits and about one-third of the total industrial and commercial work force. This trend is continuing and we can expect to see the largest 100 firms control more and more of the economy.[6] It cannot be said that this trend towards greater concentration is being stimulated only by the desire of these firms to obtain greater economies of large scale production.

Table I below summarizes the results obtained by G. N. Newbold[7] in a study of 38 mergers which took place during 1961–68.

Newbold asked the managers of the bidding firms what were the main reasons which had motivated them. It is interesting to see that 'market dominance' and 'defensive' account for almost one-half of the total.

TABLE I

Major Reasons for Merging

Reason	Relative Importance
Market Dominance	27
Defensive	21
Re-enforcement	16
Diversification	9
Financial	9
Technological/Economic	8
Others	10
Total	100

Note: Each firm was asked to allocate 10 points between the various reasons. Total number of points to be awarded therefore was 380 and 'market dominance' received 102 or 27 per cent.

Moreover, profitability does not always increase with concentration[8]; far from increasing it frequently declines with the size of firm.[9]

Finally, Chapters 5 and 6 show that the majority of firms build up their prices from their costs of production and the consumers' willingness to pay is considered as an afterthought. Thus instead of using price as an indication of what the consumer requires, firms in general place greater importance on other factors, i.e. their costs, in determining their output plans.

7. Factors of production are mobile

An entrepreneur cannot move into and out of markets and industries as the theory suggests. His plant and equipment are going to be relatively specialized, his managers and labour force have been trained and have experience of a particular industry. Who will purchase his existing equipment so that he can re-invest in new machines? How are the problems of labour mobility, vertical and horizontal, going to be solved? Factors of production can be mobile but the time of adjustment can be extremely long.

8. Equal distribution of income

The allocation of resources would only be optimum if the distribution of income was equal. The price mechanism will allocate resources according to the strength of demand and in an economy where few are rich and the majority poor it is likely that a disproportionate amount of resources are devoted to meeting the needs of a small percentage of the population.

In Britain the top 1 per cent of income earners command 8 per cent of total pretax incomes. The top 10 per cent receive approximately 28 per cent of total incomes. At the other end of the scale, the poorest 20 per cent of British families get only $7\frac{1}{2}$ per cent of the national income.

When we look at the ownership of wealth the inequality is even greater: the top 1 per cent wealth holders own 29 per cent of the total personal wealth in the country. The top 5 per cent own over half the total.

9. No public or national goods

The provision of public goods or national goods, e.g. schools; roads, hospitals, defence, etc., cannot be left to the price mechanism and therefore the central government and local authorities must interfere to some extent with market forces to provide these goods in sufficient quantity. How could the price mechanism cope with defence expenditure? It must be provided collectively. Some people would not be prepared to pay anything while others would value it. Yet if a war broke out how would the armed forces distinguish who has paid, and who has not, and who is to be defended?

10. No divergence between private and social costs and benefits[10]

In taking decisions whether or not to produce, firms will take into account costs which appear on their financial statements. These costs (private), however, are not necessarily all the costs and for the decision to lead to an optimum solution the relevant social costs must be included. For example, to close down a factory in a region which already has a high degree of unemployment may be justified on commercial grounds but from the national viewpoint keeping the factory open may be justified because the factors of production cannot be used elsewhere in the region and would remain unproductive.

18

11. Mixed economy

For all these reasons there exists in most economies some degree of state intervention designed to correct the distortions introduced into economic activity by imperfections of competition or the maldistribution of income (see Chapter 8 for government intervention) or to make provision for needs of a social, strategic or a political nature.

The price mechanism has a part to play; to go to the other extreme of a 'command economy' produces distortions on a grand scale; the example of the Soviet Union given below illustrates the impracticality of attempting to plan absolutely everything that is to take place in the economy. The determination of a price that reflects relative scarcity (opportunity cost) is essential.

The problem is not a choice between one extreme and the other (free play of market forces and command economy) but a question of what sort of mix do we want. How much state intervention is desired is largely a matter of personal judgement although society as a whole must arrive at its conclusions.

A COMMAND ECONOMY

12. Aims and strategy

The Soviet Union has been the scene of an industrial and social as well as of a political revolution. Great changes have been compressed into a short time, and these changes have been carried through under the leadership of the Communist Party which has transformed a backward peasant country into a giant industrial power. This involved the tearing asunder of established ways of life, and indeed other systematic disregard of the pressure of existing economic forces.

Soviet policy makers did not seek to adapt themselves to the demand patterns; the point was to change the demand pattern, the institutions, and the structure of the economy. The economy was deliberately so organized as to facilitate this drastic and complex process, and this led to the neglect not only of non-priority sectors of economic life, but also the finer adjustments required for 'optimal' resource allocation. Professor Oscar Lange[11] has described this stage of Soviet development as a 'war economy' in the sense of an all out concentration of effort on a major objective determined by political authority.

It must always be borne in mind that Soviet institutions were created to serve certain purposes; that many of the problems are intimately connected with and are often part of the cost of the pursuit of rapid industrialization in a backward country, and that it is not always useful to criticize the Soviet economic system as if its aims were to achieve the pure static equilibrium of western textbooks.

After the Revolution the leaders, particularly Stalin, saw Russia as a poor, backward, vulnerable agrarian country surrounded by hostile capitalist states and their main objectives were the attainment of industrial and military power as quickly as possible. This is the reason why central planning became so important; they could not afford to let the market allocate resources to industries that were not regarded by them as being priority.

The priority sector was heavy industry which meant iron and steel, heavy engineering, electric power generation, mining, and more recently chemicals. To concentrate on heavy industry as much as they did meant the neglect of other sectors of industry such as communications, light engineering, and consumer good industries. The result of pursuing this strategy was 'forced growth' and 'unbalanced growth'.[12]

13. Material balances[13]

The market mechanism could not be relied upon to achieve the aims established by the leaders of the Revolution and so prices were relegated to a secondary role as a means of allocating resources and central planning took its place.

The Central Planning Commission (Gosplan) was to make decisions regarding virtually everything. The priority sectors had been chosen and Gosplan had to decide for the coming year what output they were to achieve, how much investment they required, their total needs with regard to labour, raw materials, power, finance, etc.

To draw up such a plan they used the material balance system. These material balances determine supply and demand for major products, commodities and factors of production, the aim being to match total demand for every major resource against its available supply in the absence of markets and a flexible price system.

The planning is carried out mainly in quantitative terms, target outputs being derived from technical coefficients which were originally derived themselves from past experience and technical knowledge. One of the main purposes of material balances is to look for bottlenecks in the economy and, if these bottlenecks exist in a priority sector, then an investment drive or campaign is instigated to remedy the situation.

14. Problems of planning accurately by means of material balances

These problems can be divided into two groups:

(1) Failure in the transmission to higher authorities of information about the production functions of individual producers, and,

(2) errors that come to light in the process of fulfilling the plan.

Taking the first problem above, the knowledge which planners in Gosplan have of the relevant input co-efficients may be inaccurate for a number of reasons:

(a) Technical norms are often unrealistic to start with, since they usually assume a quality of material inputs and conditions of repair and maintenance of equipment which are not normally met in practice. They may also hinge on the above average performance of the workers operating the materials-consuming equipment.
(b) Many norms at the plant level are ignored because the complexities of the production processes and the frequently changing specification of the products render them useless for planning purposes.
(c) Due to rapid technical progress, it is not possible to keep all the norms up to date.
(d) The norms are often poorly aggregated even at the level of the enterprise.
(e) The quotas of materials earmarked for repairs and maintenance are liable to a wide margin of error.
(f) The output mix of an industry is frequently so complex that material needs can only be gauged in proportion to the gross value of output to the industry or of a group of products rather than for each of the products separately.

Turning now to our second general problem, it is very possible that many unforeseen contingencies may cause production and consumption plans to go awry in the course of their fulfilment:

(a) Changes in the demand for finished products ordered by the authorities during the year; political events such as war scares may require a new system of material balances. Quotas earmarked for one purpose may be pre-empted for another which will upset the fulfilment of enterprise plans.

(b) Producers frequently fail to notify consumers of production breakdowns, and the latter are left with no alternative sources of supply.

(c) Above plan output will require additional materials which will call for a myriad of lower level decisions which may or may not be in harmony with the central plan.

(d) Certain industrial consumers are allotted supplies from the production of new factories scheduled to be opened during the year. But it is difficult to fix an exact date for the start of full scale operations in new factories. Consumers are, therefore, at the mercy of these completion dates. Shortfalls in deliveries will upset their own outplans which in turn will have repercussions in the rest of the economy.

Therefore, relegating prices to secondary importance and ignoring market forces created enormous problems for the Soviets. The fact that prices were state-controlled and were not allowed to reflect scarcity and opportunity cost meant that profits and the profit motive also played a very small part in the allocation of resources.

The industrial prices were based on average cost of production, but in keeping with Marx's theory of value, average cost did not include a charge for rent or interest. Inter-industry prices were regarded as being relatively unimportant because basically there was no change of ownership, yet without taking into account all charges, efficiency between plans was difficult to measure and the allocation of resources for investment purposes became very haphazard.

15. The lack of an effective profit motive[14]

The function of the Soviet manager is to see that his enterprise carries out efficiently the tasks assigned to it by the 'plan'. Among these tasks the fulfilment of the output target, as a rule, has been considered uppermost in importance, and substantial premiums await the director whose enterprise fulfils and over-fulfils the output plan. Other success indicators have been incorporated into the system such as cost reduction, but incentive premiums for fulfilment or over-fulfilment of any indices are always contingent upon the fulfilment of the output plan.

As an incentive to management performance, profit has been of minor significance, mainly because it has not been used as a source of premium for rewarding enterprise managers.

This system of managerial bonuses, however, often leads to a misallocation of resources, for it fails in many respects to make the personal interests of the enterprise managers coincide with the interests of the economy.

The shortcomings of the system are as follows:

(a) Enterprise managers are induced to hide productive capacity. Since the fulfilment and the over-fulfilment of the quantitative output plan provide the major source of extra income for Soviet managers, the enterprise director has a personal stake in concealing the productive capabilities of his enterprise in order to secure the assignment of an output that can easily be fulfilled.

(b) Hoard capital. The major problem of the enterprise managers is the acquisition of equipment and resources necessary for uninterrupted production. Once they have been allocated resources they received these without interest charges. Therefore to ensure they meet their targets there is a tendency for managers to over-subscribe for capital equipment and raw materials.

(c) Built-in bias against innovations. Technological improvement may lead to greater efficiency, but the Soviet director who introduces new inventions into his enterprise runs great risk and has little to gain. Introducing new processes takes time and effort and can usually be undertaken only at the expense of a temporary decrease in production.

(d) Wrong goods are produced. Unless an enterprise produces a commodity which is easily identifiable, it is an impossible task for Gosplan to specify exactly what is to be produced by everyone in relation to size, quality, quantity, etc. For success to be measured, however, the target plan must be defined by some measure which can be weight, value, length, area, etc. In almost all cases, however, distortions and illogicalities result in the course of the plan fulfilment at the enterprise level. When the output target is in tons, then any shift to a less heavy variant will be avoided; when the measure of success has been in money terms it has for example discouraged the production of cheap goods. The use of 'value added' as a success indicator encourages the maximum amount of work to be carried out within the enterprise and discourages the rational forms of inter-enterprise co-operation and sub-contracting.

The basic difficulty has always been the absence of any objective criterion for price fixing, and the lack of a logical relationship between prices, profits and the desired assortment of production.

16. Reform
Since the death of Stalin in 1953 many economists have openly criticized the system and have suggested reforms which would amount to de-centralization of decision-making; the use of market forces in certain sectors of the economy to determine prices; the re-appraisal of the method of setting industrial prices, i.e. introduction of a notional interest charge so that investment appraisal and efficiency comparisons can be made.

Many of these ideas have been associated with F. Liberman although the degree of de-centralization and price flexibility he proposes is open to discussion. The fact that the economy has become larger and more complex, the multiplication of priorities and the increasing scarcity of factors of production, has brought the old system of material balances under severe criticism.

Reforms have been applied initially in the consumer goods sector although how far they will spread is more a political rather than an economic question.

17. Conclusion
Enough has been said above to demonstrate that we cannot rely on the forces of the market or on total central planning to allocate resources in the most efficient manner. We must not come to the conclusion that all is chaos in the Soviet Union: this is far from

the case especially with the introduction of reforms, yet the waste of scarce resources which we are trying to highlight is clear.

It is interesting that at the same time as reforms in the Soviet Union are leading to greater de-centralization most Western governments are playing a larger role in their economies than ever before.

REFERENCES

1. Adam Smith, *Wealth of Nations*, 18.
2. Consumer Association.
3. *National Income and Expenditure 1967*, Central Statistical Office, H.M.S.O., extracted from table 27.
4. A. P. Lerner, 'The Economics and Politics of Consumer Sovereignty', *A.E.R. P. & P.*, May 1972.
5. Peter Donaldson, *Economics of the Real World*, Pelican, 1972.
6. *Financial Times*, 21 March 1973, 'Constraints on Corporate Growth'.
7. G. D. Newbold, *Management and Merger Activity*, Guthstead, 1970.
8. Singh and Whittington, *Growth Profitability and Valuation*, C.U.P., 1968.
9. J. M. Samuels and D. Smyth, *Economica*, May 1968.
10. For a more detailed study of the price mechanism see forthcoming in this series: Roy Thomas, *The Price Mechanism and Cost Benefit Analysis*.
11. Oscar Lange, *The Political Economy of Socialism*, Warsaw, 1957.
12. 'Forced growth'. There is no exact definition for this term but what it means very generally is that compulsion was introduced into all aspects of life. People were told where and when to work, firms were told what to produce and how much to produce. In addition, the rapid growth was achieved through great sacrifice on the population, e.g. 25 per cent of the National Income was invested and used for accumulation purposes.
    'Unbalanced Growth'. This is the logical result of a strategy which gives priority to some sectors at the expense of others and gives rise to the constant formation of bottlenecks.
13. J. M. Montias, 'Planning with Material Balances', *A.E.R.*, 1959.
14. Alec Nove, *Was Stalin Really Necessary?* Allen and Unwin, 1964.
    Alec Nove, *The Soviet Economy*, Allen and Unwin, 1969.

PROGRESS TEST

1. Explain the mechanism through which entrepreneurs motivated by the desire to maximize profits achieve an optimum allocation of resources. (1, 2, 3)
2. Why are factors of production not as mobile as is suggested by perfect competition? Explain what is meant by vertical and horizontal mobility in labour. (7)
3. What trends have taken place in the economy in relation to industrial structure that threaten consumer sovereignty? (5, 6)
4. Explain the terms 'forced growth' and 'unbalanced growth'.
5. Describe the problems incurred in planning an economy through a system of material balances. (13, 14)
6. Why has the Soviet Union found it necessary to introduce the profit motive into certain sectors of the economy? (15, 16)

3 THE ANALYSIS OF COSTS FOR PRICING DECISIONS

1. Introduction

The analysis of costs plays a central role in aiding management to make decisions. Every decision requires a comparison between what extra benefits will be derived by the firm against the additional costs that will have to be incurred in carrying out the action. In determining the price of a product or service, correct cost analysis is essential, although as will be shown in Chapter 5 a knowledge of the costs that will be incurred in carrying out an action is merely the first step in price determination.[1]

The determination of a price involves the consideration of many factors other than cost. To say this is not to underestimate the importance of costs, but merely to look upon costs in their proper perspective. In the past too much emphasis has been placed on the importance of costs, and worse, incorrect cost concepts have been used.

2. Incremental cost

For decision-making, the costs to be taken into consideration should be only those costs that are going to be incurred as a direct result of taking that decision. If a particular cost is unchanged by a given decision, the incremental cost for the action undertaken is zero. Although this description of incremental cost seems straightforward, its application in practice involves great care because consideration must be given to: costs which do not appear in the profit and loss account; the long-run effects of the decision; and also the price that has been paid for factors of production currently owned by the firm which cannot be taken and used without serious consideration.

Taking these points in turn, the first point means that opportunity cost must be considered. By opportunity cost is meant that the cost of using an asset is the most profitable alternative foregone because the asset is employed in its present use rather than for something else. For example a business should charge itself for the use of its own money because if it had not been utilized in the business, at the very least it could be earning interest in a bank account. On the other hand, take the example of a highly specialized machine that has no alternative use but a book value of £10,000. The opportunity cost of using that machine is zero because it has no alternative use.

Turning to the second point, unless the long-run implications of a decision are considered there is a danger that the calculated incremental costs will be too low. For example, a firm accepts an order in a period of depressed business at a price which exceeds the short-run incremental cost, but is insufficiently high to cover its total cost. Business very soon recovers and the firm's previous customers who have been paying higher prices return. Very soon the firm finds itself in a situation where it is working at full capacity and unless it acquires extra capacity (increases its commitment of fixed cost) it will have to turn away profitable business. The firm now realizes it has not taken into account the long-run effects of accepting the contract in the depressed period. If the firm is not prepared to invest and increase its capacity, then the long-run incremental cost in accepting the original order would be the extra profit which will have to remain unearned due to lack of capacity to meet the more profitable orders. If they had been prepared to increase capacity through purchasing extra machinery or making additions to the factory space, then the decision to accept the order and the future orders which were expected to arise would have to be made with the aid of investment appraisal techniques. It is at this stage that additions to fixed costs should be considered, when there is control over whether they are to be incurred or not. Once the decision to incur them has been taken, they become a sunk cost – a cost which has to be met by the firm regardless of the level of output.

The third point is important because firms do not buy factors of production and use them immediately. If they did, then cost would mean the price paid for a factor. However, when items are purchased and stored and, even more complicated, when a fixed asset is used over a period of years, what then is the cost of using such assets? Historical costs may in these cases be unimportant and, if used, misleading. Take for example a furniture factory that purchases lengths of timber at 25p per foot and has stocks to the value of £1,000. The price of timber increases to 50p per foot and the firm is making a quotation for a contract; what cost should it use? The answer is the present cost per foot because it would cost the firm £2,000 to replace its stocks and also it could sell the wood on the open market for 50p per foot.

To apply the concept of incremental cost in practice, in addition to the points made above, it must also be possible to:

(a) classify the costs faced by the firm into the categories of fixed and variable, and
(b) predict how the firm's cost will behave with variations in activity.

Practitioners are wary of using the incremental cost concept because of the fear that prices will be set too low and total costs will not be fully covered. It must be emphasized, however, that what we are trying to do with the aid of the incremental cost concept is to determine the true cost of taking a decision. The costs which are arrived at are merely a base to work from – a bench mark. The price that will be charged will depend on the relative strengths of the various factors mentioned in Chapters 5 and 6.

3. Cost classification

To carry out production a firm needs to employ a variety of factors of production: unskilled and skilled labour; raw materials; land; public services, etc. These factors must be paid for to compensate them for their contribution, and basic economic theory has classified these costs into two major categories: fixed cost and variable cost. Fixed costs represent costs that are unrelated to the volume of output. A decision was made in the past to incur them and a charge will be made on the firm regardless of the level of output, e.g. rent; rates; supervisors' salaries; etc. Variable cost represents costs that are directly related to output, e.g. direct wages; heating; materials; power; spoilage; wear and tear on equipment.

The above classifications, however, are only relevant when the time period of the decision is specified. Economic theory distinguishes between the short run and the long run. By the short

29

run is meant that period of time during which capacity cannot be increased or decreased. By the long run is meant that period of time during which capacity can be so increased or decreased. No calendar time can be placed on these periods. The length of the short run varies according to the industry. The more technical and complicated and unique the factors of production required, the longer the short period. For example, compare training machine operatives on an assembly line with training doctors, accountants or pilots.

Therefore, what is fixed and what is variable depends upon the time period being considered because in the long run all costs are variable. In practice the distinction between the short and long run is not so clear cut; the periods tend to shade into one another as minor adjustments are continually being made, carrying the firm into the long run and then into a new short-run situation. A firm is really in a constant state of long-run adaption.

4. Cost behaviour

Figure I below shows how the average cost per unit of producing a particular commodity varies over the production capacity of that firm. Average fixed cost (AFC) falls continuously as output is increased because the fixed cost is being spread over a greater number of units.

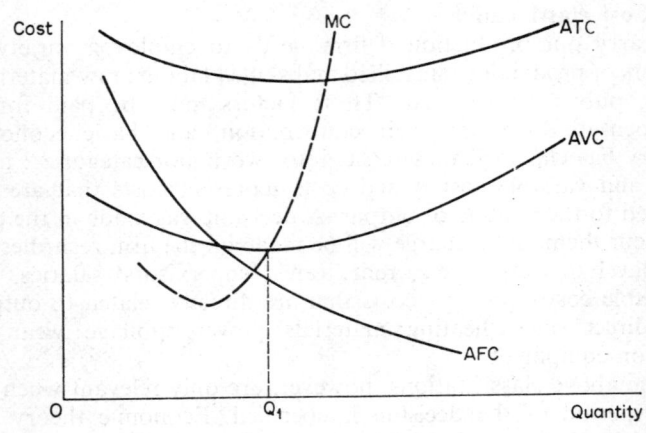

FIG I

Average variable cost (AVC) is U shaped reflecting the firm's production function. The production function specifies the technical relationship between combinations of inputs and the level of output, and this factor, combined with the prices of inputs determines the cost function.

The left-hand portion of the AVC curve continues to fall because of the existence of increasing returns. As the output of the firm increases AVC falls because the factors of production are being combined in a more efficient manner and the firm is operating closer and closer to the optimum output for which it was designed.

Output can increase beyond Q, but AVC now starts to increase. The factors of production are being combined in a less efficient manner and diminishing returns result. The main cause of diminishing returns is the fixity of factor supply, i.e. plant and equipment, and the attempt to add more and more of the variable factors to the existing fixed factors, e.g. to increase output men are asked to work overtime. However, in many cases they are paid twice the normal hourly rate for doing so; maintenance periods have to be omitted which increases wear and tear on the machinery; because the men are working longer hours, they are not as efficient as previously, mistakes occur more often, spoilage increases.

Marginal cost (MC) is the cost incurred in producing one more unit of output.

Average total cost (ATC) is obtained through adding together the AVC and AFC curves.

5.   The importance of correct classification

Establishing the correct time scale for a decision will mean that a classification of what is a fixed cost and what is a variable cost can be made. Understanding what 'additional costs' are going to be incurred by an action is essential for making a decision with regard to price and output.

Although a firm must recover all of its costs in the long run to remain in business, it is essential to recognize that the only costs that are relevant in making a decision are the costs that are going to be influenced by that decision. In Figure II below, if price is at P1 then the firm will recover all of its costs and there is no problem. If, however, price falls to P2 although revenue is

31

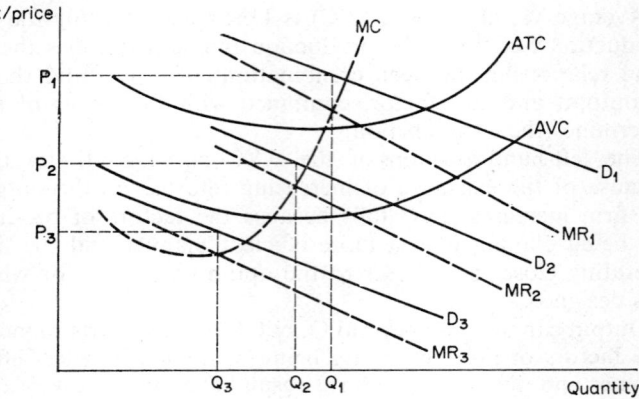

FIG II

insufficient to cover total cost it will be worthwhile for the firm
to accept the price and continue production until it can adjust its
capacity and lower the level of its FC. Fixed costs are irrelevant
for this problem because they will have to be incurred regardless
of the level of output. As long as price exceeds AVC then a
contribution is being made towards the FC. It is only when price
falls to P3 would it be correct to cease production because in
those circumstances the firm would be making a loss on every
unit it produced in addition to the FC it already incurs.

6. Problems of applying economic theory in practice
We shall now consider three problem areas that make the selection of the relevant costs difficult in practice.

(a) The difficulty of identifying what is fixed and what is variable.
(b) The accountant's use of information.
(c) The difference between the accountant and the economist as
    to how costs will behave with variations in output.

7. Identifying fixed and variable costs

(a) The dividing line between what is a Fixed Cost and what is a
    Variable Cost is not the same for all decisions. Let us take,

32

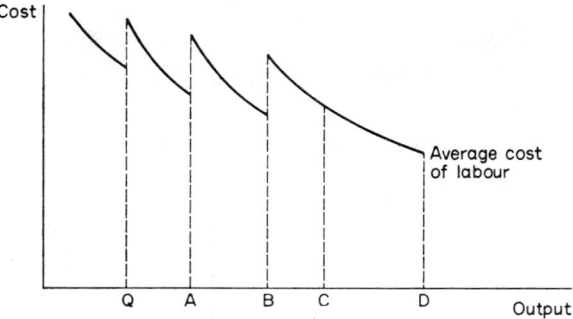

FIG III

for example, direct labour cost. It makes a difference whether a decision to accept a particular order requires the addition of overtime or can be managed with the use of available idle time. With regard to direct labour, D. A. Saunders has referred to the 'ratchet effect' operating in the short run 'whereby Variable Costs in total are not reduced as output decreases because management is reluctant to lay off workers. But for increases in output they are a variable cost'.[2]

In Figure III above, as output falls from OD to OC direct labour is still employed in quantities that is only justified by output OD. However, if output continues to fall, say to OB, then labour will be released. It follows that just as there are a variety of short runs there are a variety of ways in which expenses can be segregated into fixed and variable categories. The decision maker must select the classification suited to his purpose.

(b) It is also wrong to assume that an expense must be either fixed or variable. They can be semi-fixed or semi-variable. Bierman[3] differentiates these terms according to which aspect predominates.

Depreciation is composed of two parts – wear and tear (variable) and obsolescence (fixed period costs). Other examples of semi-fixed and semi-variable costs are electricity, gas and telephone charges which can include a fixed charge

33

and a charge based on consumption. In the same way, salesmen can be paid on a salary plus bonus depending on sales.

Figure IV below shows how these various categories of cost vary with activity.

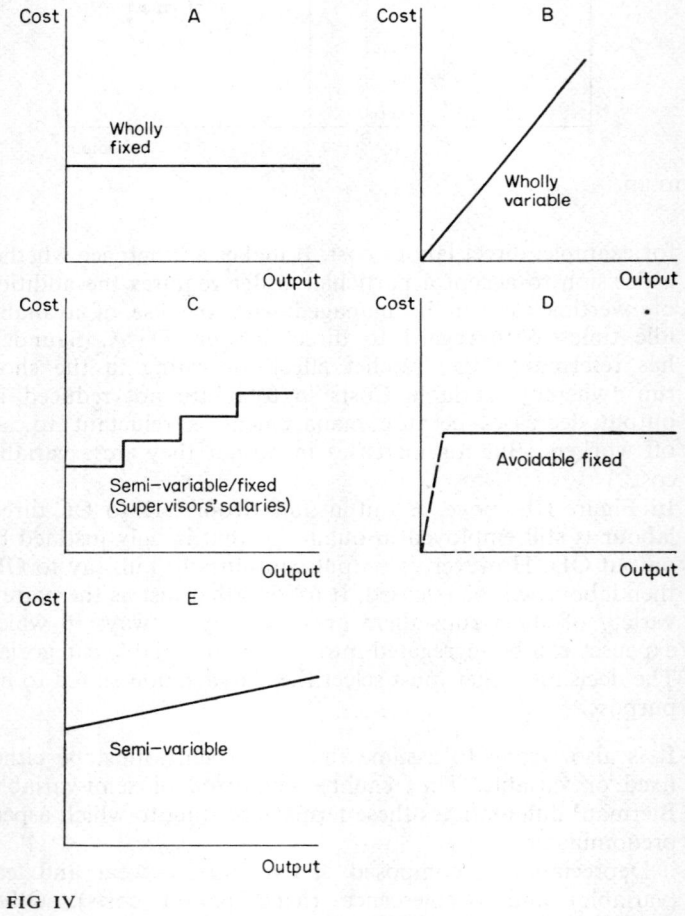

FIG IV

In practice various methods exist to determine the fixed and variable components of a certain expense. These methods vary from using an accounting classification, where everything is either fixed or variable, to engineering estimates and to the use of statistical methods. There is no one approach which is superior to others, it being a question of deciding which is the most suitable for the costs under consideration. 'Many of the methods which are used by accountants to separate the variable element are open to criticism. . . . The approach of some accountants is too rigid and inflexible. They tend to make a one-for-all classification of costs as fixed and variable, and frequently use unadjusted historical data.'[4]

To illustrate the use of one of these methods let us look at an example of the determination of fixed and variable cost by the use of one of the more simple statistical methods that merely compares a high level of activity with a low level of activity:

Owain owns a small factory producing engineering components. Table II below compares the cost of maintenance of the machinery in his factory with the output produced in the last six periods.

TABLE II

Cost of Maintenance

Period	Total Cost (£)	Output (units)
1	300	40
2	395	60
3	450	70
4	365	55
5	330	45
6	372	58

To separate the fixed and variable components of the total cost we need to compare the highest and lowest levels of activity and assume that the cost difference is purely variable and incurred directly through increased production. Applying the variable cost per unit to our high and low outputs enables us to establish the fixed element of the total cost:

	Output	*Total Cost*
Period 3	70	450
Period 1	40	300

Variable Cost per unit $= \dfrac{150}{30} = $ £5

Fixed Cost period 1 $= 300 - (40 \times 5) = $ £100

or

Fixed Cost period 3 $= 450 - (70 \times 5) = $ £100

Although more sophisticated statistical techniques can be employed, e.g. regression or multiple regression analysis, the results must be interpreted with caution. There are numerous factors in addition to volume which cause costs to vary; also, in practice, there is a tendency for the accountant to use unadjusted historic data and assume that all other factors are constant during the period to which this data relates.

(c) The expression 'completely fixed expense' is open to various interpretations and we need to distinguish among the following kinds of fixed cost.

  (i) Costs which are fixed so long as operations continue, but which are escapable if operations are shut down, e.g. salaries of supervisory staff.

  (ii) Costs which run on even if production is halted, but which are escapable if the company is liquidated, e.g. heating to prevent damage to machinery and equipment, and security.

  (iii) Costs which are at the discretion of the management. Examples are advertising, research and development expenditure, and consultants' fees. These expenses go under the names of 'programmed fixed costs' or 'discretionary expenses'.

8. The accountant's use of information

If one requires information within a firm relating to costs and revenues, then the management accountant is the man to see. Unfortunately, the information that he has collected, in most cases, is better used for control purposes than decision making. Sometimes, it is possible for misunderstanding to arise over the use of jargon between an accountant and an economist and there are occasions when the accountant's direct and indirect costs have been thought to be the same as the economist's variable and fixed cost.

The accountant's terms relate to traceability. If a cost can be traced to a specific source, then that source will be credited with it regardless of whether it is fixed or variable. Overheads, therefore, are untraceable costs which can be either fixed or variable. If a firm produces only one product then all costs incurred by that firm will be attributable to that product and an ATC curve can be drawn. On the other hand, if firms produce more than one product, which is usually the case in practice, the drawing of an ATC curve becomes extremely difficult, if not impossible, because of the existence of common costs.

These common costs relate to expenses which cannot be traceable directly to any one product, e.g. sales department, maintenance, general rent and rates, general manager's salary, depreciation of buildings, general machinery, etc. Accounting practice has developed many ways of allocating and apportioning these common costs, such as on the basis of machine hours utilized, floor area utilized, direct labour cost, sales value, etc.; yet each method is likely to provide a different answer as to what is the unit cost of a product. Therefore, depending upon the method used, different decisions will be taken with regard to expanding or contracting output and even dropping entirely a product from the existing range.

The whole process of cost allotment normally passes through the following phases:[5]

(a) Allocation of whole items of cost directly associated with cost centres.
(b) Apportionment of overheads to departments on the basis of some 'plausible underlying rule of causation'[6] (primary apportionment).
(c) Re-allotment of service department costs (including those apportioned in (b) above) to production departments and possibly to other service departments (secondary apportionment).
(d) Absorption from production departments to jobs or products on a basis deemed to be the most equitable.

This whole process not only fails to distinguish between what is fixed and what is variable but also uses a number of arbitrary allotment procedures to share out the common costs.[7] These common costs are important and it is vital to the continued operation of the firm in the long run that all costs should be covered, yet for the purpose of making decisions – in a time period when the costs that are already being incurred are sunk – misleading results can emerge from attempting to allot every expense on a unit basis.

In the example that follows a firm is producing four products A, B, C and D and the fixed cost is £800. In the short run when the fixed cost cannot be changed, it would be foolish to drop any product because they all make a net contribution. In the long run, however, it may be possible by dropping product A to reduce fixed cost by £200. This decision would be worth while because in doing so the firm's profit would be increased by £100.

If we had allocated the fixed cost before making our decision, on the basis of units produced, we would be seriously considering whether to drop products A and B.

Product	A	B	C	D
Units produced	100	100	100	100
Variable Cost	400	300	200	100
Fixed Cost	200	200	200	200
	600	500	400	300
Average Cost	6	5	4	3
Selling Price	5	5	5	5
Profit/Loss per unit	(1)	–	1	2
Total Profit/Loss	(100)	–	100	200

Net Profit   £200

If we look at only the costs directly affected by the current decision to continue production we obtain the following picture. Each product provides a positive net contribution to set against the fixed cost of £800 which has to be incurred in the short run regardless of how many of the product lines are produced; to cease production of any one of these product lines, results in a fall in total contribution and total profit.

Product	A	B	C	D
Units produced	100	100	100	100
Variable Cost	400	300	200	100
Variable Cost per unit	4	3	2	1
Selling Price	5	5	5	5
Contribution per unit	1	2	3	4
Total Contribution per unit	100	200	300	400

Total Contribution £1,000 – Fixed Cost £800
Net Profit £200

The allocation and apportionment of joint costs may be justified on organizational grounds but 'there cannot be a "correct" method of apportioning joint costs and for decision purposes the main criticism levelled against them is that, by appearing to give a degree of precision to these costs which they do not possess, product decisions are made in isolation without realizing the complementary effects which they will have.'[8]

9. Difference between the accountant and the economist as to how costs will behave with variations in output

We have described in section 4 above how the economist predicts costs will behave as output is increased. The accountant, unlike the economist, assumes that AVC is linear and therefore there is no distinction between AVC and MC.

Figure V below compares the two points of view.

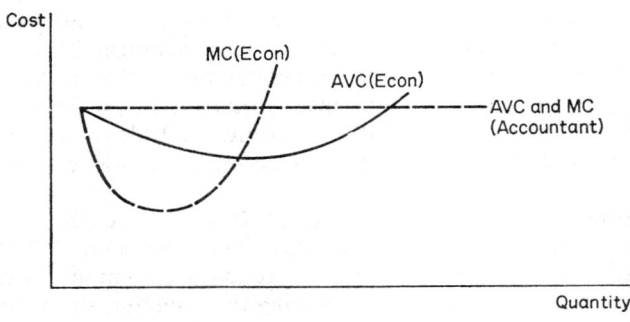

FIG V

The empirical studies[9] which have taken place in this area seem to support the views of accounting theory '. . . . the various short-run studies more often than not indicate constant marginal cost and declining average cost as the pattern that best seems to describe the data that has been analysed.'[10]

The fact that statistical studies support the linear model has not ended the controversy about the shape of the short-run cost curve. Theorists have been unwilling to abandon the law of diminishing returns which implies an increase in MC. They have noted a number of deficiencies in the statistical studies, claiming that the methods employed impart a bias towards linearity.

Stigler[11] has introduced the useful concepts of divisibility and adaptability in this connection. The orthodox economic theory rests on the assumption that the capital equipment or other fixed facilities are indivisible, but highly adaptable. By indivisible is meant that one must use the entire capital facilities or none. By adaptable is meant that facilities can be combined with varying quantities of variable inputs such as labour and materials. Under indivisible and adaptable conditions the addition of variable inputs must result in diminishing returns and rising marginal cost.

Stigler suggests that a great deal of modern manufacturing is carried out under quite different conditions. The capital equipment is often divisible but not adaptable, e.g. a textile mill. Under such conditions a doubling of output means the use of twice as many machines with double the amount of labour and materials. Output can be increased at constant MC until the capacity of the plant is reached.

The statistical studies suggest that a large portion of industry operates under such conditions of divisibility with limited adaptability, the result being linear costs within a range. This means that the AVC curve has a much greater range of constant cost (see Figure VI below) and for capacity utilization, say for example between 60 per cent and 100 per cent, variable costs will be constant and the opinion of both accountants and economists coincide.

Another economist[12] has attempted to resolve the conflict between theory and statistical evidence by proposing that the term output is two dimensional, relating to both volume and rate of activity. Accepting this, and redefining the long and short runs in terms of long and short production runs it can be shown that

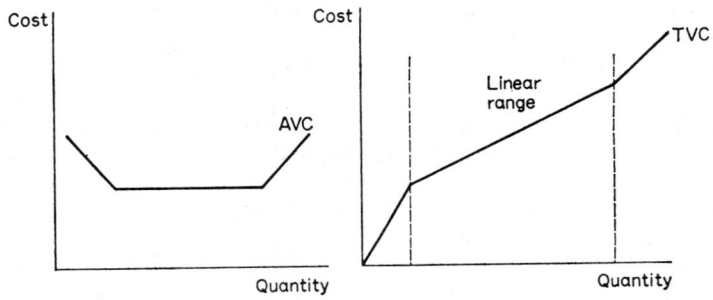

FIG VI

'marginal costs are a rising function of the rate of production, a declining function of the volume of production'.[13]

10. Additional problems

In addition to the understanding, classifying and analysis of a firm's costs which have been discussed above, the accuracy with which a firm's future costs can be estimated will depend upon a number of factors:

(a) If the product in question has been supplied by the firm for some time, then costs which have been incurred in the past will provide an invaluable guide. If on the other hand the product is new to the firm, cost estimation will be far more difficult. If the product is new to the firm, but not new to the industry then some guidelines will exist; but if the product is a new product concept then no guidelines will exist. Figures will be available from the development project and pilot studies, but practice has shown only too often that the costs incurred in proceeding to full production can be vastly different from extrapolation of pilot study results. In addition, if the product is one that involves new technology then the uncertainty increases the examples of Concorde and the Rolls Royce RB211 are illustrative here. In 1961 estimated development costs for Concorde were £150m., but after being revised many times the 1974 revision predicts £1,500m. In 1968 Rolls Royce estimated that it could develop the RB211 engine for approximately £50m., but by 1970 estimated development costs had increased to approximately £115m., and in 1971 when the company went bankrupt a re-estimation had placed the cost at £215m.

(b) Uncertainty will exist even when the product is not completely new to the firm. It may, for example, re-design the production of an article in such a way that it becomes possible for work that was previously undertaken by skilled female labour on non-automatic machines to be undertaken in the future by less skilled female labour on fully-automatic machines. Although the quantity of labour and the pace of the machines are known, the wages required to attract sufficient labour will be unknown.

(c) The uncertainty of demand forecasting, particularly for new products, means that firms are uncertain about the level of activity at which they will be operating.

11. Conclusion

The fact that many costs incurred by a firm are fixed and un-affected by the level of output makes it essential that the correct cost concept should be used in determining costs for use in aiding a decision. The costs arrived at through the use of incremental analysis are, however, merely a bench-mark to work from. For long-run survival a firm must cover all of its costs, yet to include all costs incurred to aid decision-making will lead to distorted results, because traditional absorption costing does not distinguish between fixed and variable costs and also attempts, by many arbitrary ways, to allocate common costs.

The implementation of the incremental cost concept in practice is difficult, yet these difficulties must be overcome. 'There can obviously be no single purpose cost; what we should be looking for is the particular cost which is relevant to the situation envisaged; this will seldom be based on a unit cost computed on a "full cost" basis.'[14]

REFERENCES

1. R. A. Anthony, 'What should Costs Mean?' *Harvard Business Review*, May/June 1970, pp. 121–31.

2. D. A. Saunders, 'Cost Behaviour', *Management Accounting*, Vol. 46, No. 8, August 1968, p. 344.

3. H. Bierman, *Topics in Cost Accounting and Decisions*, McGraw Hill, 1963.

4. John Sizer, *An Insight into Management Accounting*, Pelican, 1972, p. 333.
    John Sizer, 'The Determination of Fixed and Variable Costs – a Critical Appraisal', *The Accountant*, 8, 15 and 22 October, 1966.
5. H. Hart, *Overhead Costs – Analysis and Control*, Heinemann, 1973, p. 26.
6. Hart, op. cit., p. 28.
7. P. D. Wiles, *Price Cost and Output*, Basil Blackwell, 1961.
8. C. I. Savage and J. R. Small, *Introduction to Managerial Economics*, Hutchinson University Library, 1970, Chapter 6, p. 122.
9. J. Johnson, *Statistical Cost Analysis*, McGraw Hill, 1960.
10. Joel Dean, *Managerial Economics*, Prentice-Hall.
11. G. Stigler, 'Production and Distribution in the Short Run', *Journal of Political Economy*, June 1939.
12. J. Hirschleifer, 'The Firm's Cost Function: A Successful Reconstruction', *The Journal of Business*, July 1962.
13. Hirschleifer, op. cit.
14. Hart, op. cit., p. 179.

PROGRESS TEST

1. Why is it necessary to distinguish between fixed and variable costs? (2, 3, 4, 5)
2. Why is the time period important in distinguishing between a fixed and variable cost for a particular decision? (3)
3. Give examples of the items of cost that give use to the cost patterns in the figure below.

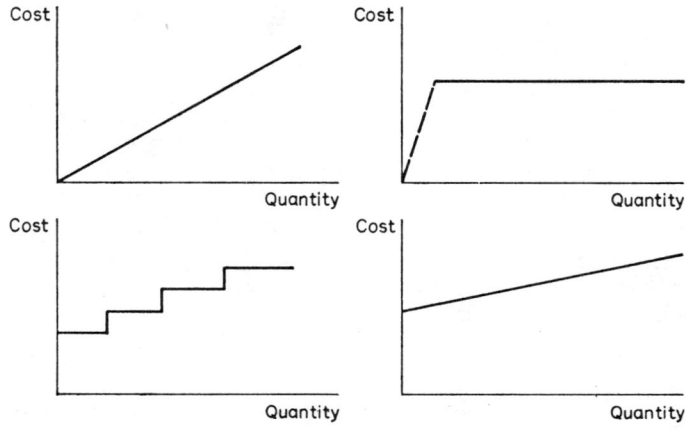

4. Do costs fall conveniently into the categories of fixed and variable? (7)

5. The figures below relate to a textile firm producing a variety of cloths. Total fixed costs per annum are £900,000 and total output of all cloths is 900,000 yards. Fixed cost is distributed on the basis of yards produced. The figures relate to cloths X, Y and Z which are produced on specialized machinery that cannot be adapted for use in producing any other cloth. The firm at present produces and sells 100,000 yards of cloths X, Y and Z at a price of £3·25 per yard. If price was lowered to £3·00 it could increase sales to 200,000 yards. On the basis of the figures provided should the firm lower its price and produce the extra output?

Cost per yard of cloths X, Y and Z

	100,000 yards	200,000 yards
Direct Material	0·80	0·80
Direct Labour	1·20	1·20
Spoilage	0·05	0·05
Factory Cost	2·05	2·05
General Overheads	1·00	0·90
	3·05	2·95
Selling Price	3·25	3·00

4 PRICING IN THEORY

In this chapter we propose to examine the price and output policies of firms in various market structures under conditions of comparative static equilibrium. However, we feel that concentration on price and output policy would not present a complete picture of competitive behaviour, and so in the concluding section we consider it relevant to make observations in terms of the allocational role played by profits, the existence of non-price competition, the stimulation of research and development, and the likelihood of achieving technical efficiency.

1. Demand and supply analysis

(a) *Price determination*

The traditional economic approach to price determination has centred upon the intersection of demand and supply curves. The demand and supply curves themselves represent simple functional relationships between price and output. In the diagram below the demand curve is assumed to slope downwards from left to right reflecting the fact that the lower the price the more is likely to be demanded, while the supply curve is assumed to slope upwards from left to right indicating that the higher the price the higher the amount suppliers will offer for sale. The actual price is then determined by the intersection of the demand and supply curve and this price is called the equilibrium price. It is called the equilibrium price because this is the only price at which the amount consumers are willing to purchase as shown by the demand curve is equal to the amount that producers are willing to sell as shown by the supply curve. In Figure VII OP represents the equilibrium price and OQ the equilibrium output. At any other price there will be pressure to return to the equilibrium price. For example, at price OP1 consumers will only wish to purchase OQ1 (as shown by the demand curve) while producers will want to supply OQ2 (as shown by the supply curve). This

45

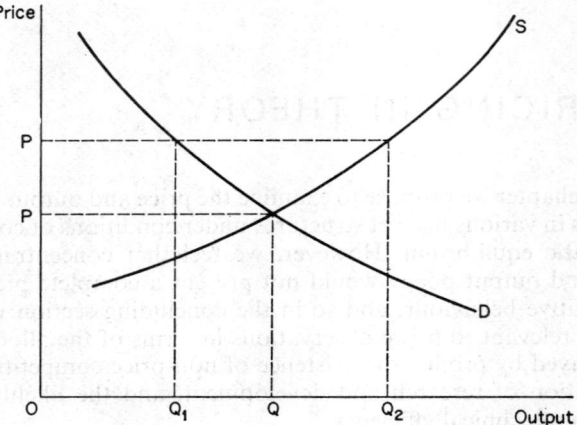

FIG VII

means that some producers will not be able to sell all their output so that there will be pressure on them to reduce their price. So long as there is excess supply (i.e. the amount offered for sale exceeds the amount demanded at that price) there will be pressure to reduce prices until the contraction in supply and the expansion in demand caused by the lower prices restores the equilibrium price. This was an example of a price above the equilibrium being restored to its equilibrium value. The reader is left to prove the converse situation of a price below the equilibrium being restored to its equilibrium value by the pressure of excess demand.

(b) *Distinction between movements along the curves and shifts in the curves*

It is extremely important to distinguish between movements along the curves caused only by changes in the price of the product itself, and shifts in the curves caused by a change in the conditions of demand and supply respectively. A movement along the demand curve simply demonstrates how the demand for the product changes as the price of the product changes (the change in price being caused by a shift of the supply curve), while a movement along the supply curve

46

demonstrates how the supply of the product changes as price changes (the change of price being caused by a shift of the demand curve). In Figure VIII below, Diagram A represents a movement along the demand curve from OQ1 to OQ2 caused by a change in price, the conditions of demand remaining unchanged. Diagram B represents a movement along the supply curve from OQ1 to OQ2 caused by a change in price, the conditions of supply remaining unchanged.

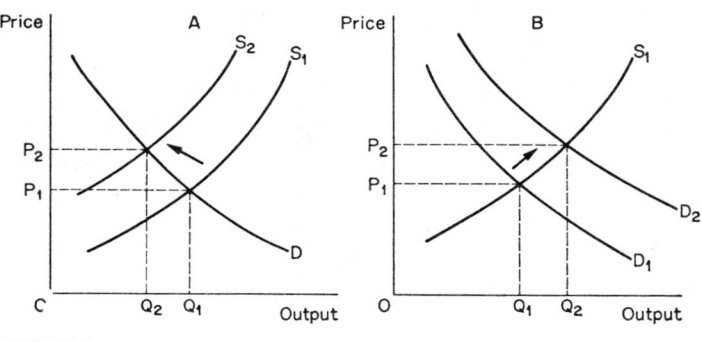

FIG VIII

Shifts in the curves, on the other hand, are caused not by changes in the price of the product but by changes in the conditions of demand or supply which are usually assumed constant when the curves are drawn up, usually expressed by the phrase *ceteris paribus* meaning other things being equal. For example, on the demand side, a shift in the demand curve may be caused by a change in the income of consumers, a change in the number of potential consumers, a change in taste, or a change in the price of other goods, particularly close substitutes or complements. Any of these changes could cause more or less to be bought at any given price, i.e. cause a shift in the demand curve. A leftward shift of the demand curve could be caused by a reduction in the income of consumers, a drop in taste for the product, a rise in the price of a complementary good (e.g. the effect of a rise in the price of petrol on the demand for cars), a fall in the price of a close substitute, or a reduction in the amount of advertising spent

47

on the product, etc. This is demonstrated in the Figure IX(a) below where the shift in the demand curve to the left from D1 to D2 has caused a fall in price and output respectively from P1 Q1 to P2 Q2. The reader is left to prove the converse; i.e. a shift to the right of the demand curve. Figure IX(b) illustrates the case of a shift downwards to the right of the supply

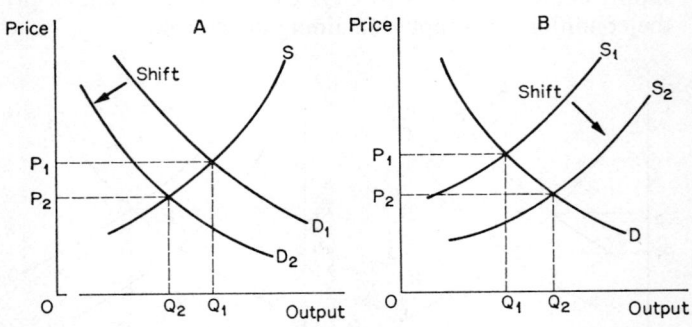

FIG IX

curve caused not by the price of the product but due possibly to a lowering of costs via new technology which may enable the firm to supply a greater output at any given price. In the diagram the shift in the supply curve from S1 to S2 caused by the new technology has brought about a lower price P2 and a higher output Q2. The reader is left to prove the converse; i.e. a leftward shift of the supply curve, produced perhaps by increased costs.

This distinction between movements along the curves and shifts in the curves have important implications for pricing behaviour. If, for example, a firm lowers the price of its product and it finds that it is now selling more than before this does not mean that the entire increase in sales is due to the lowering of price. It may be that the curves have shifted at the same time so that some of the effect may have been due to changed conditions of demand. It is for reasons such as these that firms must be particularly cautious when using observed data to forecast what its future pricing behaviour should be.

2. Criteria required for comparative static equilibrium

In order to examine pricing behaviour in any market structure, we will need first to identify average revenue, marginal revenue, average cost and marginal cost, and then apply the criteria necessary for the attainment of equilibrium. Average revenue is simply the total revenue obtained from the sale of the product divided by the number of units sold. Marginal revenue is the revenue received from the marginal unit sold, i.e. the revenue received from selling n units minus the revenue received from selling n − 1 units. Normally, the average revenue curve (which is the demand curve) will slope downwards from left to right reflecting the fact that consumers will purchase more at a lower price. In such cases the marginal revenue curve will also be downward sloping and will lie below the average revenue curve since the revenue it will earn will be the price at which it is sold minus the fall in price of all the other units of output which now have to be sold at this lower price in order to persuade the market to purchase this extra unit. (In any case if the average curve is falling then mathematically the marginal must be less than the average.) Similarly, average cost is simply the total cost of production divided by the number of units produced. Marginal cost is simply the cost of producing the marginal unit of output, i.e. the cost of producing n units minus the cost of producing n − 1 units. Economic theory generally assumes that the average cost curve will be 'U'-shaped because at first as output expands the spreading of overhead costs and the advantages of the division of labour will tend to reduce costs per unit, whereas eventually there must come a time when diminishing returns will set in caused by increased variable factors becoming less productive as they are applied to a fixed factor in the short run thus causing costs per unit to rise eventually. (The upturn in the long run is assumed to be caused by diseconomies of scale although there appears to be little empirical evidence to support this.) The marginal cost curve will be mathematically linked to the average cost curve being below the average curve when the average is falling, being above the average when the average is rising, and therefore intersecting the U-shaped average cost curve at the minimum point of the average curve.

Having derived the revenue and cost curves we then require the criteria for equilibrium both of the firm and of the industry. Equilibrium of the firm is deemed to be the position where the firm does not wish to change its price and output policy, i.e. it is maximizing its profits. This will be achieved by equating MR and MC since when MR > MC then the addition to revenue exceeds the addition to cost and it is profitable to expand output, whereas when MR > MC then the addition to revenue is less than the addition to cost, so that the profit maximizing position will be where every possible addition to profits has been taken, i.e. where MR = MC. Equilibrium of the industry is when there is neither entry to nor exit from the industry, i.e. only a normal level of profit is being earned so that there is no attraction for new firms to enter or for existing firms to leave the industry. This is achieved when AR = AC, noting that the economic definition of average cost includes a normal profit element. Thus if AR > AC then abnormal profits will attract new entry, whereas if AR < AC then less than normal profits will be earned and some firms will eventually leave the industry. Thus armed with our dual criteria of MR = MC and AR = AC we can now set about examining pricing behaviour in various market structures.

3 Pricing behaviour in perfect competition

(a) *The nature of perfect competition*

Perfect competition is a purely hypothetical situation which assumes the inability of any firm or any consumer to influence market prices. It therefore makes considerable assumptions on both the demand and the supply side. On the demand side it assumes that no single consumer can influence the market price by changing the amount of the product he purchases, that every consumer will have perfect information concerning prices throughout the market, and that every consumer will purchase the product at the lowest possible price regardless of the existence of transport costs, preference for the corner shop, etc. Similar assumptions are required on the supply side. These include the assumption that there must be a large number of sellers competing with each other; that there must be no restrictions on the entry and exit of firms into and out of the industry (i.e. that there must be no barriers to entry such as control of vital raw material supplies, product differentiation, advertising, etc.); that such entry and exit will be motivated by the level of profit being earned; that each producer and potential producer will have perfect information; and finally that each producer will be faced with a perfectly elastic supply of factors of production so that new entry will not cause such factor prices to rise.

It is not really surprising then that the sweeping assumptions of the perfectly competitive model have been widely criticized as being unrealistic and therefore that the model is irrelevant. However, the most reasoned defence of the perfectly competitive model has come from Professor Milton Friedman and the famous Chicago School of economists. They argue that a theory should be judged by the conformity of its predictions to events rather than by the conformity of its assumptions to reality. In fact Freidman argues that the more significant a theory the more unrealistic the assumptions are likely to be in that 'a hypothesis is important if it explains much by little, if it abstracts the common and crucial elements and permits valid predictions on the basis of them alone. To be important, therefore, a hypothesis must be descriptively false in its assumptions'.[1] It is not our purpose here to become involved in problems of methodology, and so we will reservedly accept the assumptions of the model and press on to examine its price/output behaviour.

(b) *Price and output determination under perfect competition*

The assumptions of the perfectly competitive model mean that the individual firm cannot influence price at all, whatever its level of output since it supplies such an infinitesimally small part of the total output of the product, i.e. the firm is a price taker with no functional relationship between price and output, so that the firm's demand curve is a horizontal line drawn through the market price. Note that since the AR (demand) curve is horizontal, the arithmetical relationship between averages and marginals also requires that the MR curve be exactly the same curve as the AR curve (i.e. since the average is constant it must be equal to the marginal).

If we now invoke our dual equilibrium criteria of MR = MC for the firm and AR = AC for the industry, the outcome will be as demonstrated in Figure X.

Since equilibrium requires both that MR = MC and AR =

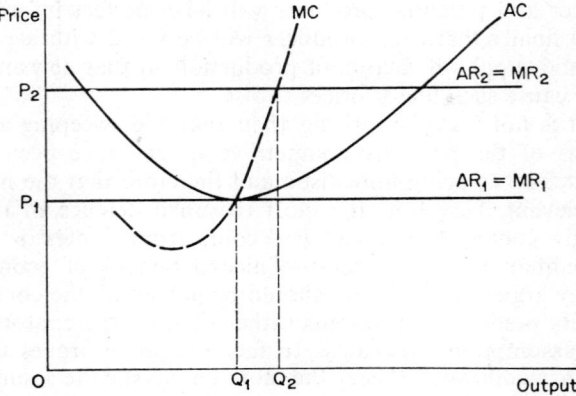

FIG X

AC and since AR = MR because the demand curve is horizontal, then both MC and AC must equal AR at the equilibrium position. But we have already proved arithmetically that MC can only equal AC at the minimum point of the AC curve. Therefore the equilibrium price and output is determined by the tangency of the AR curve to the minimum point of the AC curve, to give price OP1 and output OQ1. At any other position such as curves AR2 and MR2, the firm would be in equilibrium at price OP2 and output OQ2 (since MC = the new MR2 curve), but at that level of price and output the industry would be making abnormal profits since AR2 > AC at output OQ2, so that new firms would move into the industry lowering the individual firm's demand curve until full equilibrium is restored.

(c) *Evaluation of price output policy under perfect competition*
Price and output policy under perfect competition has two significant advantages. In the first place price is always equal to marginal cost in perfect competition, the reason being that the firm is always trying to maximize profits by equating MR and MC, and since in perfect competition AR = MR, then at the position of equilibrium AR = MC, i.e. price equals marginal cost. Thus, as can be seen in the previous diagram, in perfect competition the marginal cost curve is the supply

curve, since the equilibrium level of price and output will be determined by the intersection of the demand curve and the MC curve. Now the importance of this stems from the fact that the MC curve represents the cost of producing the marginal units of output while the price represents the amount marginal consumers are prepared to pay for the product (i.e. the price paid represents the value of the output to the marginal consumers). Thus if price was above MC, the marginal consumers would value the marginal output higher than it costs to produce, so that in order to allocate resources efficiently there is a case for extending output until the marginal worth of the product to consumers is equal to the MC of production. Conversely, if price is below MC, the cost of the marginal resources being used up exceeds their value to the community, so that production should be curtailed until price once again equals MC. Thus price = MC brings about an ideal allocation of resources.

The second significant feature of perfect competition is that in equilibrium firms will always be producing at the minimum average cost of production. This is because this is the only position in which the dual equilibrium criteria will be satisfied. Thus in perfect competition not only do we have an efficient allocation of resources but we also have an optimum factor combination in that there is neither excess capacity nor diminishing returns.

4. Pricing behaviour in monopoly

(a) *The nature of monopoly*

Monopoly is at the opposite extreme to perfect competition. It assumes that there is only one firm in the industry, and that this firm can restrict entry to the industry, thus maintaining its monopoly position in the long run.[2]

Once again it is possible to contest the assumptions of the monopoly model and argue that in practice there is a substitute (however inferior it may be) for every product, so that some competition is bound to exist. One could even take this argument to its logical conclusion and argue that in the last analysis all products are in competition for the consumer's income. However, although accepting this argument in principle, it is unquestionable that monopolistic behaviour can be observed in certain types of market structure, and it is worth noting that British monopoly policy recognizes that monopolistic investigation may be warranted when a firm's market share of a particular class of goods exceeds the 25 per cent level.

(b) *Price and output policy under monopoly*
The essential point to recognize about the theoretical monopolist is that there is only one firm in the industry so that all we need to determine the equilibrium position is the profit maximizing criterion for the firm, i.e. MR = MC. In the case of monopoly, unlike that of perfect competition, the demand curve will be of the normal downward sloping type since a 10 per cent increase in output by the firm will represent a 10 per cent increase in output by the industry, thus forcing the price down in order to sell this increase in output. The MR curve will be arithmetically linked to the AR curve as before, and the cost curves will be the normal U-shaped ones.

In Figure XI below, the equilibrium price and output will be at OP and OQ respectively (i.e. the level of output determined where MC = MR, and the price then given by the height of the demand curve vertically above this level of output). Note that at this equilibrium position AR > AC so that abnormal profits are being earned, equal in the diagram

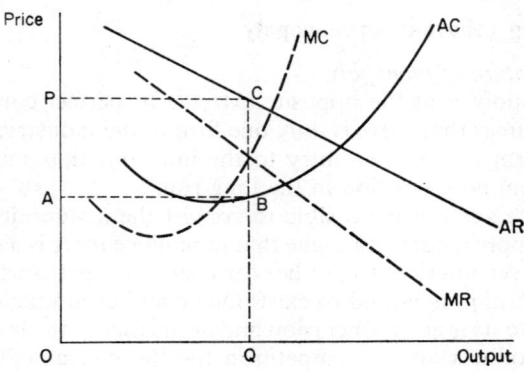

FIG XI

to area PABC. Unlike perfect competition, these abnormal profits can persist in the long-run equilibrium position since monopoly power includes the power to restrict entry to the industry so that new firms cannot enter and compete away these abnormal profits.

The important feature about the monopolist is that he can either decide the price at which he is going to sell or the output he is going to sell, but he cannot determine both. Whichever one of these he chooses the demand curve the firm is facing will determine the other. Thus the demand curve the firm is facing is of crucial importance to the monopolist, particularly if he is able to segment his market into two or more separate and isolated sections in which separate prices can be charged. This is generally referred to as price discrimination and is only possible if there is no possibility of resale between one segment and another, and most important it is only profitable if the elasticity of demand is different in each market. Thus a profit maximizing monopolist would charge a higher price in a market with an inelastic demand and a lower price in a market with an elastic demand, the actual position being where the marginal revenue in each market is equal to the marginal cost of his total output. The reader can demonstrate the importance of elasticity simply by changing the slopes of the AR and MR curves in the diagram.[3]

(c) *Evaluation of price output policy under monopoly*
In the first place price will usually be higher and output lower under monopoly than under perfect competition. The reason is obvious – the monopolist's equilibrium price and output will be determined by the intersection of MR and MC whereas in perfect competition price is determined where AR = MC. Since with a downward sloping demand curve AR does not equal MR and MR will in fact be to the left of AR, then the MC curve must intersect the MR curve before it intersects the AR curve, thus leading to a lower output and a higher price. In Figure XII the monopolist's price and output is given by PM and QM respectively and the price and output of the perfectly competitive firm are given by PC and QC respectively. Thus, if we assume that monopolists are faced by exactly the

55

same cost structures as competitive firms, then our pricing theory leads us to the conclusion that price is higher and output is lower under conditions of monopoly. Moreover, for the same reason that price equal to MC brought about a welfare optimum under conditions of perfect competition, price > MC brings about a misallocation of resources.

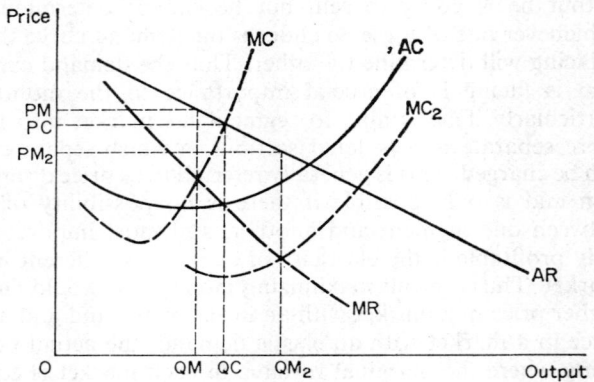

FIG XII

A second criticism of the monopolistic model is that it is unlikely, except by pure chance, that the monopolist will be operating at the minimum point of the average cost curve. In theory at least it is just as likely to be operating on the downward or upward sloping parts of the AC curve.

However, in reality, both these criticisms need to be put in their right perspective and because they are related we will consider them together. That price will be higher under monopoly than under competition rests on the assumption that the cost curves of the two market structures will be identical. The truth is that monopolists are likely to reap the benefits of economies of scale so that the monopolist is likely to have lower costs than the competitive firm. If we assume that MC2 is the new lower cost curve of the monopolist (we have omitted the corresponding AC2 curve so as not to complicate matters) then the new price and output under monopoly would be PM2 and QM2 respectively, i.e. price would be lower and output higher than under competition. Moreover, the empirical evidence relating to economies of scale suggest that there is a wide range of output over which the average cost curve is horizontal, and since there is very little evidence to suggest the existence of diseconomies of scale[4] the likelihood is that the monopolist will be operating somewhere on the horizontal part of the cost curve, i.e. at some point to the right of OQ in Figure XIII. Thus from a technical point of view a monopolist is likely to have lower costs than a competitive firm.

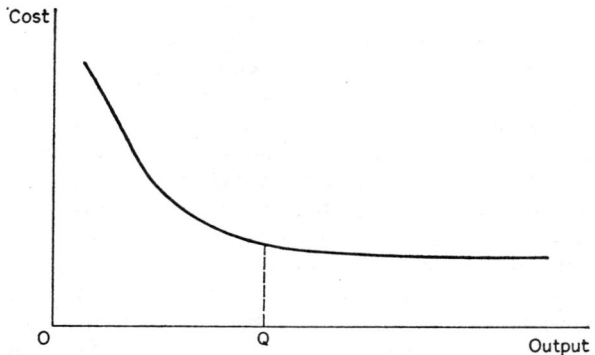

FIG XIII

Thus from a purely static, pricing point of view, whether or not one finds monopoly acceptable depends upon the assumptions one makes about cost curves. In this respect it is worth noting that in recent years a more fearful shadow has loomed upon the horizon in the shape of the X inefficiency concept, whose very existence threatens to eat up all the benefits of economies of scale. We will return to these problems in Chapter 8 when we discuss government regulation of market structure.

5. Pricing behaviour in imperfect competition

(a) *The nature of imperfect competition*

Imperfect competition, along with oligopoly which we will consider in the next section, is generally regarded as the type of competition that exists in the real world. On the supply side there are several producers who can considerably influence the total supply of changes in their output, and are thus in a position to have some influence upon price. In a sense each producer is a monopolist since each firm has a monopoly of its own product, but on the other hand, each firm is facing the competition of other brands. Thus, what we have is a group of producers whose products are fairly close substitutes, and whose markets are not isolated from each other.

The situation described above poses considerable problems for determination of a group equilibrium position. In the first place, on the demand side each individual firm within the group has its own individual product with its own distinctive features and qualitative differences, and consequently its own individual demand curve which differs from that of all other firms. Similarly, on the supply side, the product of each firm is slightly differentiated from each other firm in the group, but this degree of differentiation varies from firm to firm, so that some firms are 'closer' to others in terms of product differentiation and are more likely to be influenced by the firms 'nearest' to them in terms of product differentiation.

In order to obtain an equilibrium position Chamberlin[5] found it necessary to make 'heroic' assumptions. In the first place he found it necessary to make the famous uniformity assumption that both demand and cost curves for all the products are uniform throughout the group. This assumption required that consumers' preferences be evenly distributed among the different products. The other major assumption was the famous symmetry assumption that any adjustment of price or of product by a single producer spreads its influence over so many of his competitors that the impact felt by any one firm is negligible and does not lead any other firm into a readjustment of its own situation. Once again, it is possible to attack the realism of these assumptions,[6] but as in the case of the other market structures it is more fruitful to pursue the

Friedmanite approach and proceed to examine the price and output determination process.

(b) *Price and output determination in imperfect competition*
In imperfect competition the cost curves will be of the normal U-shape, and the demand curve will be of the normal downward-sloping type since each firm is in a position to influence the market price by altering its supply. We will require equilibrium of both the firm and the industry and so we will need our dual criteria of MR = MC and AR = AC respectively. The sweeping assumptions made in the model enable the tangency solution where AR is tangential to AC to bring about the dual equilibrium of both firm and industry at the same level of price and output. Figure XIV is similar to the monopoly equilibrium diagram, the difference being that in

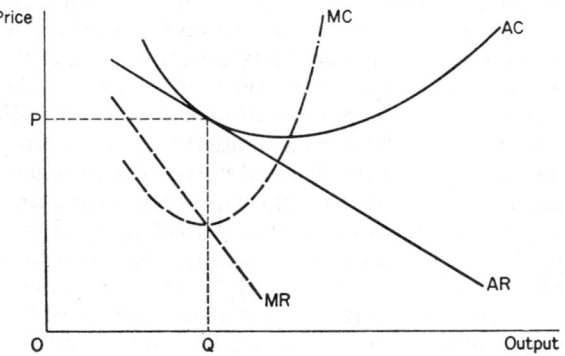

FIG XIV

imperfect competition the abnormal profits are all competed away by the entry of new firms, such new entry continuing until only normal profits are earned, i.e. new entry causes the demand curve for the individual firm to shift to the left until there are no abnormal profits left to attract entry, i.e. until the AR curve is tangential to the AC curve. Mathematically, the tangency solution with AR = AC also means that MR = MC at output OQ, since to the left of Q, AC is falling more rapidly than AR (so that MC must be less than MR) while to the right of Q, AC is falling less rapidly than

59

AR (so that MC must be greater than MR) so that where the slope of AR = AC then MR must equal MC. Thus the equilibrium price and output in imperfect competition will be OP and OQ respectively.

(c) *Evaluation of price and output policy under imperfect competition*

In the first place, like monopoly, the equilibrium level of price and output is determined by the intersection of MR and MC and with a downward sloping demand curve this means that price will be higher and output lower than in perfect competition where AR = MC. Thus imperfect competition does not bring about an ideal allocation of resources since price exceeds MC.

In comparison with monopoly it could be argued that imperfect competition does not permit the existence of abnormal profits in the long run. However, this is a direct result of the uniformity and symmetry assumptions and if these do not hold then the equilibrium position for any one firm could be similar to the monopoly position in that product differentiation enables some firms to insulate themselves from potential competition so that the demand curve no longer moves back all the way to provide the tangency solution. Indeed, it could be argued that most firms in imperfect competition attempt via product differentiation, advertising, etc., both to shift their individual demand curve to the right and make it more inelastic. However, once we pursue this avenue of thought we no longer have a determinate equilibrium for the group.

In so far as the cost curves are concerned note that the equilibrium position means that the firms in the group are not operating at minimum average cost, and are in fact operating on the downward part of the AC curve so that they are not reaping the full benefits of economies of scale. This is the famous 'excess capacity' result of imperfectly competitive equilibrium, meaning that each firm in the group has some degree of unused capacity. If one adds to this the wastes of competitive advertising, which most firms indulge in and which to a large extent therefore cancels itself out, then imperfect competition does not augur well for the cost side of the analysis either.

6. Pricing behaviour in oligopoly

(a) *The nature of oligopoly*

Oligopoly has been described by the term 'competition among the few'. It is characterized by a situation in which because there are only a few firms, each will produce a significant proportion of the industry's output, and consequently each firm will be in a position to influence the price of the product by changing its output. Similarly, each firm will be buying a significant proportion of the factors of production used in the industry and consequently is in a position to influence factor prices. However, the major problem so far as price determination is concerned is that any action taken by one firm significantly affects the other firms in the industry who may in turn react to protect their positions in the industry. In other words, any reduction in price by Oligopolist X will increase its sales partly from the extension of demand for the product at the lower price and partly at the expense of its rivals. Thus firm X will not know how much it can increase its sales by a reduction in price without knowing how its rivals will react. Thus the firm cannot know its demand curve without making some assumptions about the reaction of its rivals. Similar difficulties arise in the purchase of factors of production. Thus oligopoly is characterized by a situation in which individual firms' demand curves and supply schedules cannot be identified without making assumptions about the reactions of rivals. These features considerably complicate the price/output determination process to which we will now turn.

(b) *Price and output determination under oligopoly*

If it is impossible to define either a demand function or a supply function for an individual firm because of the existence of interdependence between firms, then it is obvious that a determinate equilibrium in the usual sense is not possible unless we make further assumptions about the reaction functions of firms. Either it is assumed that oligopolists do not take account of the effects of their actions on the policies of their rivals, as in the famous Cournot and Bertrand solutions,[7] or certain types of reaction functions are assumed such as the firms affected respond merely in a way that maximizes their profits. Alternatively, it could be assumed that oligopolists attempt to maximize the joint profits of the group. It is obvious then that a whole host of solutions are possible depending upon what assumptions one wants to make as to possible reaction functions.

Since we have analysed all the other market structures in terms of profit maximization, we will concentrate on the possibility of achieving a joint profit maximizing solution to the oligopoly problem. Note that if such a solution were to be achieved then the outcome so far as price and output policy is concerned would be similar to that under monopoly. The actual outcome is likely to be a tendency towards the maximization of the joint profits of the group. Fellner[8] suggests that traditional value theory sets the limits within which bargaining takes place, the upper limit for each firm being set by the possibility of obtaining for itself the entire joint profit, while the lower limit for each firm is at the zero profit level. Within these bargaining ranges Fellner suggests that the actual outcome will depend upon the following factors: the long-run consequences of violating accepted value judgements (i.e. the ability of firms to convince the public that they are not taking advantage of their positions); the immediate political consequences of a stalemate in the relations between the firms (i.e. whether a firm thinks it will benefit more from administrative regulation rather than regulation by market forces) will determine its attitude towards extended cut-throat competition and the inevitable political intervention; the ability of firms to take losses and to inflict losses on other firms during a period of intense competition; and finally the relative toughness of firms in the sense of their unwillingness to yield to their competitors. Fellner suggests that on the whole one can expect an equilibrium position to be reached as a result of such bargaining.

However, there are a number of reasons why we are not likely to get complete maximization of the joint profits of the group.

i. The existence of cut-throat competition. This phrase is used to describe a situation in which firms fix prices with the objective of forcing their competitors into a change of policy, rather than with the objective of maximizing immediate profits. This policy will reduce the profits of all firms in the industry in the short run and may even involve them in losses, but may be regarded as worth while if it enables a firm to eliminate some of its rivals or reduce their bargaining strength. Cut-throat competition performs the function of testing the strength of firms from time to time. For example, the last case of cut-throat competition in the detergent industry was in 1955, since when there has been virtually no price competition.

ii. The impact of changes in the economic environment. The understanding between firms is likely to be an extremely nebulous one and firms will be reluctant to undertake policies which a rival can take advantage of in the light of a break-down in the agreement. This is why prices tend to be fairly rigid in oligopolistic market structures and provides an explanation of the 'kinked' demand curve. In Figure XV below once the price is fixed at OP there is a reluctance to change it. There is a reluctance for any individual firm to raise prices about OP in case the other firms do not do likewise, in which case the demand curve about OP will be very elastic and the firm will lose a large part of its market. Conversely, if any firms were to reduce price below OP other firms would follow in order to protect their market shares so that the demand curve below OP would be extremely inelastic providing no incentive to reduce price. This rigidity is likely to make prices slow to respond to changing environmental conditions.

iii. The influence of different cost curves. The price that will

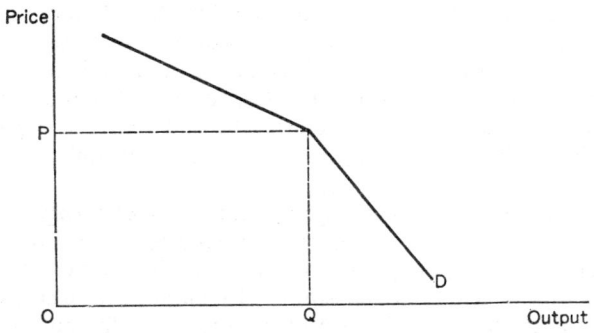

FIG XV

PRICING IN PRACTICE

achieve joint profit maximization is unlikely to bring about an acceptable distribution of that profit. In Figure XVI below if we assume that firm A has 50 per cent of the market and firm B has 50 per cent of the market, but that firm B has lower costs than firm A, then we can see that firm A would prefer price P1, firm B price P2, whereas joint profit maximization would require a price of P3. Which of these outcomes will prevail will depend upon the bargaining strengths of the firms involved. In the absence of an extremely firm agreement, it is unlikely that the joint profits maximization solution will be achieved with some agreed distribution of profits.

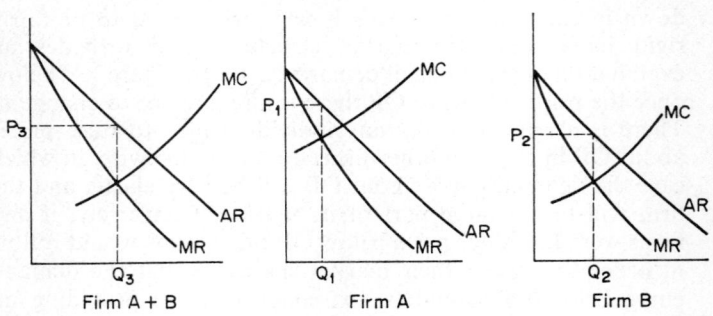

FIG XVI

iv. The existence of non-price competition. The maximization of joint profits would require severe restrictions upon advertising expenditure, product differentiation and other forms of non-price competition. It is unlikely that oligopolistic firms would agree to such restrictions since they regard active manipulation of these variables as representing the best chance of improving their relative bargaining position in the long run.

(c) *Evaluation of price and output policy under oligopoly*
It has already been stated in the preceding section that in the event of a tendency towards joint profit maximization the outcome is likely to be similar to monopoly. Certainly we would expect the existence of abnormal profits and also AR well in excess of MC so that an optimum allocation is not

achieved. It is in fact possible if high-cost firms are in a strong bargaining position that industry output could actually be lower and price higher than in monopoly (e.g. compare the price of firm A in the preceding diagram with that of the joint-profit maximizing solution), although in general we would expect the low-cost firms to be in a better bargaining position so that price would be lower and output higher than in a monopoly (e.g. compare the price of firm B with that of the joint-profit maximizing solution).

Moreover, we would expect this tendency towards a lower price than monopoly to be enhanced by the greater effect that potential competition has in oligopolistic market structures. It is true that oligopolists are to some extent protected from the full force of potential competition by economies of scale, product differentiation and other barriers to entry,[9] but nevertheless, in most cases they are forced to set a price low enough to forestall entry (the reader is referred to Bain's *Barriers to New Competition* for a full discussion of the effects of potential competition).

In so far as cost curves are concerned most oligopolists are large enough to take full advantage of economies of scale, the empirical evidence suggesting that most oligopolists are on the horizontal part of the long-run cost curve. However, the existence of non-price competition in the form of advertising,[10] product differentiation, after-sales service, etc., is likely to raise the cost curve higher than it need be.

Nevertheless, oligopolistic competition is a different kind of competition from competition among the many. It is characterized not so much by price, but rather by quality, cost reduction and technical progress. It is worth noting that very rapid progress has been made in a number of industries in which this type of structure prevails.

7. Conclusion

Perfect competition is the only market structure which achieves both an optimum allocation of the goods already produced (via the marginal cost pricing rule) and also guides new investment to its most efficient use (via the generation and elimination of short-run abnormal profits). All other. types of market structure fall considerably short of this in that they all produce pricing solutions in excess of marginal cost and most of them (monopoly and oligopoly) inhibit the allocational function of the profit mechanism in that institutional forces prevent the elimination of abnormal profits. Thus on purely allocational grounds the perfectly competitive mechanism reigns supreme.

However, once we consider the cost side of the equation the balance begins to tip the other way. It is true that perfect competition achieves an optimum factor combination (i.e. operates at the minimum point of the average cost curve) for the equilibrium level of output of the firm, but the problem is that this level of output is likely to be too small to take advantage of economies of scale. Thus, even imperfect competition with its excess capacity problem (i.e. operating on the falling part of the average cost curve) is likely to have lower costs per unit of output than perfect competition because its firms may be able to take some advantage of the economies of scale.[11] Once we consider oligopoly and monopoly the case becomes overwhelming. It is true that oligopolists suffer from the excessive costs of non-price competition and it may be true that large firms suffer from the cost disadvantages of X inefficiency (for a fuller explanation see Chapter 8), but even so the economies of scale which these firms reap are likely to outweigh by far these extra costs. Thus, from a purely cost point of view, the argument supports the more concentrated market structures.

Moreover, if we move from purely static comparisons to include more dynamic elements such as promotion of research and development, the case against perfect competition and in favour of more concentrated market structures improves considerably. Despite the inconclusive debate concerning the *a priori* relationship between market structure and research and development, the empirical evidence points overwhelmingly to positive association between both firm size and market structure. Perhaps the most significant finding was that of a 'threshold' effect,[12] below which size, firms were too small to be able to commit resources to a large-scale research and development effort.

Where then does this leave us? It would seem that even if we wanted perfect competition, a piecemeal approach in which we proceeded to break firms up industry by industry might not lead us any nearer the welfare optimum because of the existence of 'second best'[13] problems. Perhaps, in the last analysis, government legislation designed to curb the more undesirable excesses of concentrated market structures may enable us to have the best of both worlds.

REFERENCES

1. M. Friedman, *Essays in Positive Economics*, Chicago University Press, 1953, Chapter 1.
2. D. Lee, V. Anthony and A. Skuse, *Monopoly*, Heinemann (Studies in the British Economy), 1972.
3. See Chapter 5, sections 19, 20 and 21.
4. D. Needham, *Economic Analysis and Industrial Structure*, Holt, Rinehart and Winston, 1969, Chapter 3.
5. E. Chamberlin, *Theory of Monopolistic Competition*, Oxford University Press, 8th edition, 1962, Chapter 5.
6. G. C. Archibald, 'Chamberlin versus Chicago', *Review of Economic Studies*, 1961/2.
7. See W. Fellner, *Competition Among the Few*, Kelley, 1960, Chapter 2.
8. Fellner, op. cit., Chapter 1.
9. J. S. Bain, *Barriers to New Competition*, Harvard University Press, 1956.
10. E. Savage, *Advertising*, Heinemann (Studies in the British Economy), 1971.
11. H. Demsetz, *The Nature of Equilibrium in Monopolistic Competition J.P.E.*, 1959.
12. F. M. Scherer, *Industrial Market Structure and Economic Performance*, Rand McNally, 1970, Chapter 15.
13. R. G. Lipsey and K. Lancaster, 'The General Theory of Second Best', *Review of Economic Studies*, 1956.

PROGRESS TEST

1. Why is it necessary to distinguish between movements along the demand curve and shifts in the demand curve? (1b)
2. What is meant by equilibrium of the firm and of the industry? What are the criteria for achieving equilibrium? (2)
3. What assumptions are made in perfect competition, imperfect competition, monopoly and oligopoly? Does it matter if these assumptions are unrealistic? (3a, 4a, 5a, 6a)

4. Do abnormal profits always arise with a downward sloping demand curve? (4b, 5b, 6b)
5. Does perfect competition lead to an ideal allocation of resources? (3b, 3c, 7)
6. What conditions are necessary for profitable price discrimination? (4b)
7. Does monopoly lead to a higher price and a lower output than (i) perfect competition, (ii) imperfect competition, (iii) oligopoly? (4c, 5b, 5c, 6b, 6c)
8. Why does imperfect competition lead to excess capacity? (5a, 5b, 5c)
9. Why is price often said to be indeterminate in oligopoly? (6a, 6b, 6c)
10. Why does oligopoly lead to price rigidity and non-price competition? (6a, 6b, 6c)

5 PRICING IN PRACTICE

1. Limitations of economic theory

All the theories of pricing behaviour which were looked at in the last chapter, with the exception of oligopoly, fall under the heading of marginalism. All of them assume an entrepreneur who weighs the penalties and rewards of pricing decisions. He compares the added gain and added cost of increasing output, or of changing price, and works towards the position at which the added gain and loss are equal.

We accept the viewpoint of marginalism as a useful way of organizing one's thoughts about pricing decisions, but at the same time the managerial economist must learn to distinguish between what the traditional theory can and cannot do. The theory suffers from serious limitations when it comes to the analysis of individual firm behaviour.

(a) The theory usually rests on the assumption of profit maximization. In the real world no doubt profit maximization is a primary objective, but research indicates clearly that entrepreneurs are guided by other motives (see Chapter 1).

(b) The theory does not distinguish clearly between the long and short-run effects of price change. Putting the matter in another way, traditional economic theory does not deal adequately with the dynamics of pricing. In particular, the theory has little to say about the effect of today's prices on future profits. The usual graphs for short-run pricing show today's demand curve and today's cost curves and suggest that the manager prices to equate marginal revenue and marginal cost. The manager may, however, try to consider the discounted effect of today's price on future revenues, e.g. if he wants to build up an image of a low-price outlet he may avoid charging as much as the immediate market would permit, sacrificing current profits for future profits.

(c) The theory usually assumes a single product firm. The real world is made up of firms producing several products.

(d) The theory does not face up to the problem of uncertainty. Economic theory assumes that the entrepreneur knows his demand and cost functions, yet in the world of business this is hardly ever the case.

(e) The theory fails to view the firm as an organization in which pricing decisions are influenced by a variety of persons with varied objectives and motives within and outside the firm; for example Alfred R. Oxenfeldt[1] lists seven main parties to the pricing process: those responsible for sales promotion; the ultimate customer of the product; rival sellers; potential rivals; middlemen; suppliers; and government. Economic theory usually stresses only two of these parties: the buyers and the sellers. (Oligopoly is the exception and places a great deal of emphasis on potential competition.) The pricing process in practice must take all of them into account for they all are involved in the pattern of communications and influence which determines the final outcome.

2. Full cost pricing
Research has indicated that in practice some form of full cost pricing or cost plus pricing is frequently employed. By this method a price is arrived at mainly from the cost side of the equation by adding to variable cost a proportion of the firm's overheads (the proportion being absorbed by each unit depends upon what level of normal output has been established for the year, e.g. total overheads £1m. and normal output for the year is assumed at 500,000 units. Therefore, each unit shoulders £2 of the overheads) and then adding to this a percentage mark up for profit.

$$\text{Selling price} = \text{VC} + \text{FC} + \% \text{ mark up}$$
$$\pounds 6.60 \qquad = (\pounds 4) + (\pounds 2) + 10\%$$

3. A criticism of full cost pricing
The major criticism of this form of pricing has already been made in Chapter 3, i.e.

(a) it is impossible in practice correctly to allocate overheads among different products;

(b) the total costs of conventional absorption costing are not costs that are good for decision making. Incremental costs are required, the additional cost which would result from the change in volume.

Establishing a price on the above basis contains dangers in that if these average total costs are regarded as the benchmark for price making, business which is going at a price which is less than total unit cost, but which nevertheless would cover the marginal cost, and make a contribution to fixed costs, may be rejected.

In Figure XVII below there has been a fall in demand indicated by the demand curve having shifted from D_1 to D_2. The price

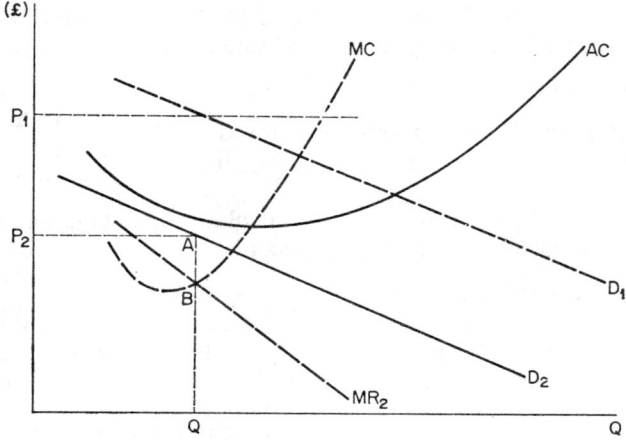

FIG XVII

level falls from P1 to P2 and the firm in the diagram can no longer cover AC. However, in the short run the firm would be unwise to refuse business at a price of P2 because although AC is not being covered the price P2 is high enough to cover MC and provide a contribution AB per unit to the FC. These costs remain the same whether the order is accepted or not. They would be justified in refusing the order only if price fell below MC because in these circumstances in addition to their FC they would be losing money for every unit produced.

71

The argument is particularly relevant when business is bad and output is low.

4. Rate of return pricing

A refinement of the basic full cost pricing we have just looked at is rate of return pricing.

In this valuation management first decides on a rate of return they would like to achieve on capital employed. To translate this rate of return into a percentage mark up on costs:

(a) normal rate of production must be estimated;
(b) total costs of a year's normal production are estimated;
(c) value of capital employed is estimated.

The ratio of normal capital employed to the year's total annual cost is then multiplied by the desired rate of return.

The formula is:

$$\text{Percentage mark up on Cost} = \frac{\text{Capital Employed}}{\text{Total Annual Cost}} \times \text{Planned Rate of Return on Capital Employed}$$

Given the figures below we can calculate percentage mark up on cost and determine the selling price:

Variable Cost	£20 per unit
Fixed Cost	£1,000,000
Normal Production	100,000 units
Normal Capital Employed:	
Variable	£5 per unit
Fixed	£2,000,000
Desired rate of return	15%

Substituting figures into the formula:

$$\frac{(100,000 \times 5) + 2,000,000}{(100,000 \times 20) + 1,000,000} \times 15$$

$$\frac{500,000 + 2}{2,000,000 + 1} \times 15 = 12\tfrac{1}{2}\%$$

Selling price per unit which will produce the desired rate of return of 15 per cent will be:

Variable Cost per unit	20
Fixed Cost per unit	10
(£1,000,000 ÷ 100,000)	
Total Cost	30
12½% Mark up	3·75
Selling Price	33·75

If variations occur in the normal rate of output then the planned rate of return will not be achieved. To take extreme cases in the above example, if output was 200,000 then rate of return would be 58·3 per cent, while if output fell to 75,000 rate of return would fall to 1·3 per cent.

The basic problem of arbitrary allocation of overheads and using the wrong cost concept for decision making still holds.

Rate of return was introduced to relate the mark up to a recognized measurement of profit but the basic problem of allocating the fixed cost remains. The refinement is misleading in that the formula gives the mark up a form of credibility which in practice leads to inflexibility in taking pricing decisions.

5. Criticism of full cost pricing

'The best that can be said for full cost pricing is that it is easy and it appears to be a safe method of pricing'.[2]

Full cost pricing has been criticized on the following grounds:

(a) It ignores demand. It fails to take account of the buyer's needs and willingness to pay, which govern the sales volume obtainable at each of a series of prices. The price that people will pay for a product bears no necessary relation to what it costs any particular manufacturer to make it.
(b) It fails to reflect competition adequately. The effect of a price upon rivals' reactions and the effect upon the birth of potential competition is omitted from this simple formula.
(c) It overplays the precision of allocated costs. (See Chapter 3 on costs.)
(d) It is based upon a concept of cost that is frequently not relevant for the pricing decision. For many decisions incremental costs rather than full costs should be controlling future

73

costs not present or historic costs. Opportunity costs, i.e. alternative uses for facilities are important, but they are not usually reflected in accounting systems.

(e) It involves circular reasoning to some degree if current full cost is used as the base. To the extent that unit costs varies with output, and thus with sales volume, this cost depends partly on the price charged, provided that demand has significant elasticity and fixed overhead cost is important.

6. Reasons for continued use of full cost pricing

Given these criticisms and the strong possibility that full cost pricing might result in a non-optimal price/output decision, why do so many businesses use full cost pricing?

Is there a rationale for its continued use by many business firms?

(a) Firms do not want to maximize profits. Prices based on full costs are thought to be 'fair' to consumers and competitors.

(b) Continued short run profit maximization may in the long run be detrimental to the firm. Actions today will lead to reactions tomorrow, therefore, because short run profit maximization is seldom consistent with long run wealth maximization, firms do not typically attempt to maximize short run profits.

(c) Price changes are costly and inconvenient to salesmen.

(d) The existence of uncertainty about the marginal relationships of the demand and cost functions make it too risky to move away from full cost pricing in practice.

(e) Considering the extra effort and expense required to produce information that would show us the marginal relationships with some degree of confidence, perhaps the extra effort required outweighs the extra profits that could be earned after their exact determination. It follows from this that 'short cut' decision techniques may actually be resulting in maximum profits when full consideration is given to the added expense of obtaining the data necessary for complete marginal analysis.

These reasons provide some explanation for the widespread use of full cost pricing, but do not justify it as the logical approach to pricing. It provides no escape from the great difficulties of cost identification and allocation previously discussed.

All the criticisms made of full cost pricing only apply when it is practised in its crudest form. In practice firms are not blind to consumers' reactions and the fact that a large percentage of firms operate under conditions of oligopoly[3] means they are extremely aware of the dangers of potential competition in addition to existing competition and therefore set their prices accordingly. (See Chapter 4 on Oligopoly Pricing.)

The structure of profit margins among different products for firms using full cost pricing provides clear evidence that demand analysis does in fact play an important role. The work of James S. Earley[4] showed that most firms he examined differentiated their mark ups for different product lines on the basis of competitive pressures and demand elasticities.

Kaplan, Dirlam and Lanzillotti[5] reported a similar finding in their study of pricing practices. There is no evidence, however, that the mark up used in full cost pricing results in optimal prices, i.e. prices that would be established by setting MR = MC.

7. The alternatives to marginalism and full cost pricing

So far in this chapter we have argued that neither the traditional theory of the firm with its high level of abstractions and generalizations, nor the widely known short cut formulas provide a complete answer to the pricing problem.

What we want to do now is to provide a general framework within which the manager can formulate a pricing policy. We want to establish a logic that can be applied to pricing problems. There is no formula; the problem of price is too difficult for one formula to suffice in all markets for all products and at all times.

To develop this logic we shall now discuss incremental analysis in pricing and the use of marginal cost pricing. They are quite closely connected although in practice in the determination of marginal costs not all of the relevant factors of incremental analysis are considered and costed.

8. Incremental analysis in pricing

The real world counterpart to marginal analysis is incremental profit analysis which deals with the relationship between the changes in revenues and costs associated with managerial decisions. The emphasis on only the costs and revenues that are actually affected by the decision ensures proper economic reasoning in decision analysis. That is, proper use of incremental profit analysis

75

results in rejecting any action that reduces profit and accepting any action that increases net profit.

The statement that incremental analysis involves only those factors which are affected by a particular decision does not mean that the concept is easy to apply. Proper use of incremental analysis requires a wide-ranging examination of the total effect of the decision.

The following points must be noted:

(a) In evaluating the cost impact of the pricing decision, the stress should be on the changes in cost rather than on average cost. Overhead allocations are irrelevant and should be ignored.

(b) The method requires attention to the long run as well as the short run impact of the decision. A decision to increase prices now may increase immediate profits, but it may gradually undermine the firm's reputation for low prices and destroy customer goodwill, or it may attract new competition.

(c) Consideration must be given to complementary relations in demand between one product and another. Any time the price decision on one item has an impact on the sale of other items, these additional effects on revenue must be evaluated.

(d) A careful evaluation of opportunity cost is required. It may first appear that a reduction in price is justified by the fact that the incremental costs are below the added revenues; however it should be determined whether the incremental costs include a full measure of any sacrifices of profit required by the decision.

(e) The incremental method means that attention must be given to demand elasticities or, more simply, price/volume relationships. The decision maker must develop some way of determining the impact of price changes on volume.

(f) Attention must be given to market structure. No estimate of (e) is possible without attention to the nature of competition.

(g) Incremental reasoning requires attention to changing business conditions. Instead of a mechanical application of formulas through good times and bad, it suggests the possibility of flexibility of prices to meet changing markets.

(h) Incremental reasoning implies the individualization of prices on the various products of a multi-product concern. It is true that mechanical formulas simplify pricing decisions, but the demand and competitive conditions facing products are likely to be diverse; rigid pricing formulas prevent adjustment to that diversity. This, however, is again a question of benefits versus costs.

Incremental analysis provides flexibility to pricing:

Cross sectional flexibility – individualization of pricing and flexibility over time – adaption of price to suit varying market conditions.

'It is more important to develop a way of reasoning about pricing than it is to learn specific rules. Correct reasoning can be tailor-made to particular circumstances, rules frequently are applied when they no longer fit.'[6]

9. Marginal cost pricing

As we have said previously a pricing decision involves planning for the future and as such it should deal solely with the anticipated revenues, expenses and capital outlays. All past outlays which give rise to fixed costs are historical and unchangeable (sunk costs).

We cost direct labour and materials, and add any other expenses which can be attributed to a particular product without arbitrary allocation, e.g. special jigs and tools. This average cost per unit sets the minimum price at which the product can be sold. Anything above this is a contribution to fixed cost plus profit.

The difference between selling price and variable cost is known as the contribution and the aim of the firm is to maximize the total contribution.

10. Maximizing total contribution

If for example selling price is £5 and variable cost £3, contribution per unit is £2. For each unit sold a £2 contribution is made towards existing fixed costs and profits. The fixed costs as we have already said are 'sunk costs', they are not influenced by the present decision. They will have to be paid whether a unit is produced or not so the objective should be to earn as much contribution as possible. This does not always mean one must maximize contribution per unit because, due to the elasticity of D existing at a particular time, total contribution can be greater with a lower contribution per unit because a greater amount is being taken by the market.

For example, assume that variable cost is £3 and the firm XYZ Ltd. is contemplating a selling price of either £5 or £7. At a price of £5, 200 will be sold giving a total contribution of £400. At a price of £7, 95 will be sold giving a total contribution of £380.

This idea of maximizing total contribution must be modified if the manufacturer concerned sells products which have interrelated demand functions. The aim then is to maximize total contribution over the whole range of products sold. The example below shows how marginal cost pricing can be more effective in taking a decision.

In an industry with a high proportion of fixed costs to total costs, and most industries are now moving towards this position, a wide range of price is now possible all of which are economical.

What is important to remember is that the calculation of the MC is only the first step. Price is not set at the level of MC. Price is determined by market demand, competition and all other market forces that are relevant. What must be determined as accurately as possible is what quantity can be sold at various prices. This information coupled with MC will then enable us to calculate total contribution and thus choose our price on that basis.

Pricing through MC could result in a higher price being set than full cost pricing. If insufficient notice was taken of market conditions and a straightforward historical mark up was applied in the calculation of price it would be overlooked that market demand was now stronger and therefore prepared to accept a higher price.

11. Example of marginal cost pricing

In the following example the Ord Co. Ltd. has a present selling price of £15 which has been in existence for a while and is now reviewing its pricing policy. MC per unit is shown for various outputs and also the results of its market research on the responsiveness of consumer demand to price changes.

TABLE III

Ord Co. Ltd.

Analysis and research provides the following figures:

MC per unit
$$0 - 1,000 = £12$$
$$1,000 - 2,000 = £10$$
$$2,000 - 5,000 = £9 \cdot 5$$
$$5,000 - 7,000 = £8$$

	Present Price		Possible Alternative Prices			
Selling Price	15	12	13	14	16	17
Estimated Annual Demand	5,000	7,000	6,500	6,000	5,700	3,000
Contribution per unit						
0 – 1,000	3	0	1	2	4	5
1,000 – 2,000	5	2	3	4	6	7
2,000 – 5,000	5·5	2·5	3·5	4·5	6·5	7·5
5,000 – 7,000	7	4	5	6	8	9
Total Contribution						
0 – 1,000	3,000	0,000	1,000	2,000	4,000	5,000
1,000 – 2,000	5,000	2,000	3,000	4,000	6,000	7,000
2,000 – 5,000	16,500	7,500	10,500	13,500	19,500	9,000
5,000 – 7,000	0,000	8,000	7,500	6,000	5,600	0,000
Total	24,500	17,500	22,000	25,500	35,100	21,000

The results of the analysis show that raising the price to £16 would provide a greater total contribution. The firm would also gain (£1,000) by lowering the price to £14. The fixed costs have not been taken into consideration because they would be the same for output ranging from 3,000 to 7,000 units. Therefore, it is not necessary to include them in the analysis at this stage. It would only be after total contribution had been established that we would introduce fixed costs to see whether our total contribution covered them and provided a satisfactory profit. Introduction of FC into the analysis before this stage would have served no purpose (see Chapter 3).

If total contribution failed to cover FC or only barely covered them and left very little profit, then a different decision would be required and that would be whether to continue to produce this product at all. If the equipment can be adapted to other uses then these channels must be explored, but if it cannot and scrap value is negligible then it would be better for the firm to continue to produce this product at a price which maximizes total contribution so that fixed costs which are continuing are being met or partially met (see example in section 3).

It is usually assumed in examples of marginal cost pricing that the firm has surplus capacity, and that additional sales can be produced without any increase in fixed costs. In reality many manufacturers are operating at less than full capacity and have L rather than U-shaped MC curves, i.e. operating below the level at which MC starts to rise. Even if the company is working at normal capacity, it can usually increase the output of the existing plant by working it more intensively. This may give rise to higher MC, but this can be taken into account when fixing prices. Bergfield, Early and Knoblock[7] show how cost volume profit analysis can cope with the problem by incorporating the new fixed costs into their calculations.

12. Advantages of marginal cost pricing

(a) The fact that most firms today operate in a number of markets with multiple products produced by a variety of processes makes the allocation of fixed costs impossible.

(b) In many businesses and in business in general as technology moves at faster rates, the dominant force is innovation and the long run situation is unpredictable. The situation can develop into a series of short runs and one must aim at maximizing contribution in each short run (see section 15).

(c) It is close to incremental analysis in its choice of costs for decision making (although it neglects opportunity cost which can be very important in the short run decision situation).

(d) It can provide better protection against potential competition than prices based on full cost; if other firms could move into our markets by switching plant and personnel from their current activities or from idleness and if they follow an incremental cost pricing policy, they may well be able to undercut our full cost prices.

13. Use of marginal cost pricing in practice

The empirical findings we have mentioned[8] show widespread use of full cost pricing regardless of the advantages of marginal cost pricing and incremental analysis. John Sizer's research[9] reveals that many firms use both full cost and marginal cost techniques. Marginal costing appears to be used for what he calls 'secondary' pricing decisions, i.e. tenders, by-products, unusual work, export orders, sub-contracting, etc., while full costs usually form the basis of the cost information provided to management for what he classifies as 'primary' decisions, for standard products sold in the home market.

It is only when 'normal' output has been achieved or is very likely to be achieved will firms consider accepting orders below their 'normal' average cost of production, or tendering for extra work on prices based on marginal cost.

The probable reasons why the full cost basis is used in 'primary' pricing decisions is because they are looked upon as being long-run decisions. When initially setting a price firms are thinking in terms of a price that will cover all their costs, and give a satisfactory rate of return in the long run. Price, of course, will be varied up or down in the future depending upon existing short run conditions.

If commitments include continuing fixed costs then managers want to see a systematic plan for recovering these costs. Absorption costing provides such a plan because each product sold contains an allowance for the fixed costs. Marginal costing offers no systematic plan, but merely points the way to maximizing contribution in the short run. It does not guarantee that all costs will be met and a normal profit will be provided in the long run. On the other hand full cost pricing only provides this guarantee if sales volume is equal to or more than normal capacity output.

We are not trying to underestimate the importance of fixed costs; on the contrary, they must be recovered in the long run if the firm is to survive. However, once one has committed resources to their creation then to include them in the analysis of the future can distort the picture. The fear of management, however, is that the emphasis on contribution might lead to accepting business which, although providing a price in excess of marginal costing, uses all the existing excess capacity so that when the opportunity arises to accept high contribution business the firm has no excess capacity.

The biggest drawback to using marginal costing is the problem of forecasting the demand curve (although this is also a problem for full cost pricing). Under these conditions of uncertainty the full cost approach is attractive to accountants; it provides a starting point from which the process of fixing selling prices can begin. As a result of this uncertainty marginal cost pricing seems to be confined to 'secondary' pricing decisions.

'Full cost pricing may save us from accepting orders which would lose money, but it will not save us from losing money through refusing, or failing to obtain orders which would have earned a margin over their incremental cost.'[10]

14. Additional considerations in price setting

The problem of pricing, as we have seen, is a very difficult one, incremental analysis and marginal cost pricing being logically superior to full cost pricing, but the fear of failing to cover fixed cost and the uncertainty of the demand function drives managers and accountants to using some variant of full cost pricing for their 'primary' pricing decisions.

As if the problem was not difficult enough, it is further complicated by a number of important factors which so far we have not considered.

It would be extremely naïve of a firm to think that once it had arrived at a price it could keep that price indefinitely or sell all its products at that price. In arriving at our final price we must ask the following questions:

(a) Do we apply it indefinitely into the future?
(Product life cycle)
(b) Do we apply this price to everyone?
(Individual negotiations)
(c) Do we apply it regardless of the quantity bought?
(Discounts)
(d) Do we apply it regardless of the time factor?
(Peak load problem)
(e) Do we apply it regardless of geography?
(Price discrimination)
(f) We must consider its effects on other products.
(Interrelationship of demand)
(g) Do we apply the price within the company?
(Transfer pricing)

15. Product life-cycle

It is recognized that all products pass through a life-cycle illustrated in Figure XVIII below. There are four stages in this cycle:
1. *The introduction stage* – when sales grow slowly because product acceptance and market awareness is low.
2. *The growth stage* – this is when sales expand rapidly as cus-

tomer awareness increases because among other things of the cumulative effect of sales promotion.

3. *The maturity stage* – the growth in sales begins to taper off although sales remain high, the potential market is now becoming exhausted.

4. *Decline* – sets in when sales begin to diminish as the product is edged out by newer or better products. Joel Dean [11] calls this process the cycle of competitive degeneration.

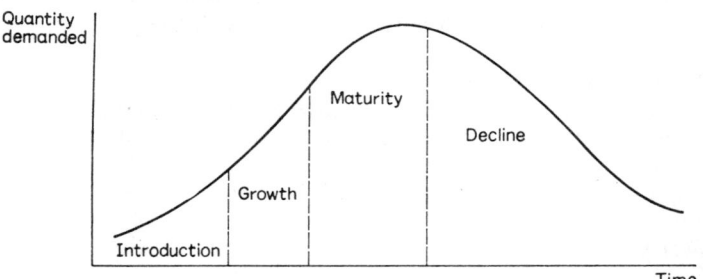

FIG XVIII

It has been shown[12] that the influence of price varies over the life-cycle of the product, i.e. the responsiveness of demand, and for a firm to achieve the maximum benefit from the resources it employs, it should deploy its competitive weapons in different proportions through the life-cycle. For example, perhaps a particular product during its introduction stage will obtain maximum consumer responsiveness by concentrating on advertising and sales promotion while in the growth stage price may lead to greater responsiveness and in maturity there should be greater emphasis on after sales service.

This point demonstrates that the firm has a number of competitive weapons at its disposal, each one varying in influence over the life-cycle of the product. Economic theory lays greatest importance on price competition whereas in many circumstances price is not the most important consideration taken into account by a potential customer. For example, in export markets to underdeveloped countries, especially for capital equipment, credit facilities and length of time to pay can be of greater importance than price.

It is fair to say that credit facilities and length of payback period are also important in the consumer durable market.

16. Individual negotiations

Many prices in industry are individually negotiated with each customer. The price to the consumer might be the same but the price to each retailer or wholesaler can vary. In fact with the growth of large chain stores, e.g. Marks and Spencer, British Home Stores, etc., producers provide products with the customers' own brands and lose virtually all identity with the product.

17. Quantity discounts

Quantity discounts are worth providing if economies of bulk buying of raw materials or any other economies of large scale production can be achieved. This point is tied up with section 16 in that large customers know if any economies are obtainable and will use the size of their order as a negotiating ploy to obtain lower prices.

18. The peak load problem

This is associated with public utilities and is discussed in depth in the chapter on nationalized industries. The private sector, however, also has peak load problems, i.e. demand for the product being uneven over a period with the result that more production capacity is required to meet the peaks than would be necessary if the demand pattern was more evenly spread.[13]

The January sales were once used to sell off old stock but nowadays firms are using the 'sales' to even out the demand for their product. The firms hope that the knowledge by the consumer of the sales that take place in January will mean that money will be held back from the Christmas shopping spree for use during January and February. Formerly January and February represented very low periods of demand and production had to be stored, which increases total production costs, in that there is more handling of the goods, and larger stores required increases in fire insurance, etc.

The tour operators who offer cheap holidays in the off-season are employing a similar strategy, although in their case they are trying to raise the demand in the off-season rather than reduce the peaks at the height of the season, although prices are varied slightly during the summer months in an attempt to spread the demand for holidays.

19. Price discrimination

We shall define price discrimination as the practice of charging prices that are not proportional to the marginal costs of slightly differentiated goods or services.

To determine whether price discrimination exists one must compare cost differentials with price differentials. The absence of price differentials may be discriminating if a product is sold for the same price over a large geographic market where transport costs must vary.

Some writers prefer the term 'differential pricing' to 'price discrimination' because the latter term is associated with monopoly and can carry special connotations.

20. Requirements for profitable price discrimination

Two conditions must apply for differential pricing to be successful:
(a) Segmentation of the market. It must be possible to segment the market and to prevent resale from one segment to another.
(b) Differences in elasticity of demand. The elasticity of demand in one segment of the market must be lower than in another, otherwise MR = MC would occur at the same price and output. Therefore nothing would be gained by segmenting the market.

Figure XIX below illustrates this pricing situation.

Demand curve for market North is in diagram A, and demand curve for market South is in diagram B. The aggregate demand curve shown in the third panel represents the horizontal sum of the quantities demanded at each price in markets North and South.

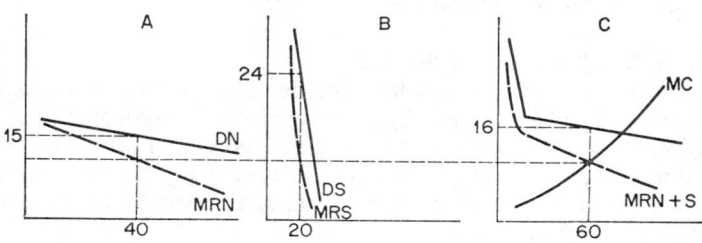

FIG XIX

From a production standpoint, it does not matter whether the product is being sold in market North or South; therefore a single marginal cost curve shown in diagram C is applicable to both markets.

> 40 units to North market at £15 each
> 20 units to South market at £24 each

The total revenue of the company is now £1,080,

$$(40 \times £15 + 20 \times £24)$$

as compared to £960 (60 × £16) if price discrimination had been impossible.

Our pricing problem can now be solved in two stages:

(a) the firm must determine the profit maximizing total output level. From the diagram C it can be seen that this is given where MC = MR N + S i.e. 60 units.
(b) the output must be allocated between the sub-markets. This is determined by drawing on the graphs a horizontal line at £10 through graphs A and B indicating that £10 is the marginal cost in each market at the indicated aggregate output.

The MC line cuts the separate marginal revenues and gives us the allocation of output.

21. Methods of price discrimination
(a) Geographic differentials. This can segment the market because transport costs make effective the prevention of resale from one market to another.
(b) Product use. Electricity is charged at different prices to industrial users and households.
(c) Age, sex and income. An example here is of the Harley Street specialist who can charge what he thinks the patient can afford. The service he offers is not resaleable.

22. Interrelationship of demand
We have said earlier that where the demand for two products is interrelated the aim should be to maximize the total contribution and not to maximize the contribution of individual products. For example, a product may be offered at cost if its sale encourages consumers to purchase other products of the firm and thus raise total contribution.

A firm may pursue a 'full line policy' when it produces and

supplies for example all sizes of writing paper and envelopes. Some of these lines are not making a great contribution, but they are not dropped and the resources transferred to the production of more profitable lines because the producer knows that distributors prefer to deal with one salesman for all his supplies. If the producer cut out a certain product line then he might find the distributor would go to another producer who can provide the full line and thus save himself time in seeing one salesman for all his needs.

23. Interrelationship in production

This arises when two or more products share common production or administration facilities or where two products are produced in one production process, e.g. sheep – wool and meat, crude oil – petroleum, paraffin and various oils for lubrication, etc.

Optimal multiple product pricing requires a complete marginal (incremental) analysis of the total effect of the decision on the firm's profitability. This analysis must include an examination of the demand interrelations of the products to be sure that a complete picture of the marginal revenue to be accrued from a decision is drawn. Likewise complementarity and competition in production must be accounted for in the analysis of marginal cost. For alternative goods produced from a common production facility, this means that opportunity cost of foregone production must be considered in determining the relevant marginal costs of a decision.

24. Transfer pricing

With the growth of firms and their division into profit centres a new pricing problem emerges. What price does one division charge another for services or goods – market prices or special preferential prices?

The answers to these questions are critically important for two reasons:

(a) The price chosen will influence the output of each division and hence the output of the firm as a whole. If the prices are not correct the firm will not produce at the optimum level.
(b) Transfer prices can be important in determining divisional profits and if promotions are based on divisional performance,

arbitrary prices charged by one division to another could have a bad effect on morale.

This topic is one of the most difficult in managerial economics and we do not propose to pursue it any further here. For further pursuance of this topic references in the bibliography provide excellent expositions of both the theoretical and the practical problems in transfer pricing.[14]

25. Pricing in open markets

Many products which a firm may produce or purchase are priced through the overall influence of aggregate demand and supply and individual firms have very little influence in setting these prices.

The products we are thinking of here are the main items dealt with on the London Commodity Markets, e.g. copper, zinc, wool, wheat, timber, etc.

Price is determined by the intersection of the aggregate demand and supply schedules. In Figure XX below price is at OP1. Forces can be set up that will shift the demand or supply curves and thus alter the equilibrium market price regardless of the actions of an individual supplier.

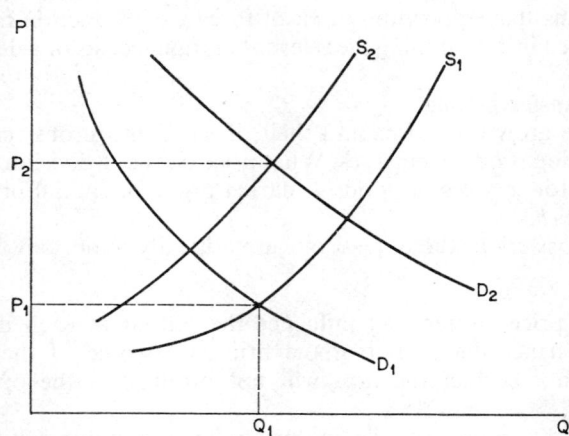

FIG XX

'There's never been anything like this in the history of the world,' a senior member of one of the biggest international grain merchants said. *'The situation today is completely out of control. It's as though a monster had got hold of the market. We can't see any end to it. As professional operators we're very scared indeed.'*

The *'international'* speculators whom Mr. Joseph Godber, Minister of Agriculture, blamed for the state of the grain market, have certainly made everyone a bit jittery.

World prices of raw materials and food crops have been rising for four and a half years. In the past 18 months they have been doing so faster than at any time since the Korean War.

The recent shakiness of the dollar has encouraged people to invest in these commodities as a hedge against devaluation. This has helped to push up prices and has now led to some panic buying.

Dealers estimate that between 9 and 10 per cent of the rise in grain prices this year can be blamed on speculators outside the trade. But speculators did not create the problem in the first place. They have been responding to a situation that already existed. It was caused, unsurprisingly, by a shortage of grain.

Until two or three years ago, there was a surplus of wheat in the world. International wheat agreements during most of the 1960s were designed to maintain a minimum price in order to protect growers.

By 1970, stocks for export had reached a peak of 64 million tons, a fifth of world production in that year. The number of acres planted with wheat was consequently reduced in the United States, Canada and Australia.

At the same time, as incomes have risen in both rich and poor countries, the demand for meat has been gradually increasing. Expanding livestock industries compete for wheat as a source of animal feed.

Another long-term influence on the international market has been the realization that the 'green revolution' in Asia will be a slower process than was once thought.

The new high-yielding varieties of wheat have fulfilled their promise of producing two or three times the yield of indigenous crops in limited areas. But for practical reasons (*because of the way in which agriculture has been organized in developing countries*) it has been difficult to increase the output of a whole country by more than an average of 20 per cent.

This trend towards greater demand and higher prices has been *distorted by a plague of natural disasters. The failure of the Russian wheat crop in 1972 was the worst of these. An exceptional winter frost was followed by an exceptional summer drought: the most disastrous weather for grain for 100 years.*

The Soviet Union bought more than 18 million tons on the world market, the largest quantity ever imported by a single country in one year. This represented more than 5·5 per cent of world wheat production and more than 30 per cent of existing world stocks. These have now fallen below 30 million tons, the lowest level for 20 years.

This coincided with increased imports into China (six million tons, twice as much as in the two preceding years), and a drought in India and South-East Asia that hit the autumn rice crop and led to renewed buying of wheat by India.

Other major crops used for animal feed have also suffered seriously: maize in sub-Saharan Africa (drought) and the Middle West and central areas of the United States (flooding); and the Peruvian anchovy catch, the world's main source of high protein fishmeal, which was more than halved by a sudden change in direction of the Humboldt Current in the Pacific, and possibly also by the effects of over-fishing in previous seasons.

The result of all this in Britain, a net grain importer, is that the price of Canadian wheat has risen from £34 to £88 a ton in the past year, and that of other crops by similarly unprecedented amounts.

Mr. Godber, unlike his Biblical namesake, could hardly be expected to foresee the lean years, but there are certain policies he could press on Britain's Common Market partners that would help to restore stability to the international market in future.

Under the old international wheat agreements, a price band was fixed. The U.S. and Canadian Governments agreed that if the price of wheat in North America fell below or rose above the limits, they would buy or sell sufficient stocks to re-establish the equilibrium.

This left other major wheat-exporting countries free to sell at fairly stable prices. The system collapsed towards the end of the 1960s, when the Americans switched to a policy of aggressive selling on the world market.

Current international wheat agreements make no provision for maintaining stable price levels, which is left to unilateral action such as the recent E.E.C. and Argentine embargoes on the export of grain.

Since most industrial countries are struggling with the problems of inflation and wage demands, which are highly responsive to food price rises, agricultural economists believe that there will be a renewed attempt during the next few months to co-ordinate stocks on an international basis.

The rise in wheat prices during 1973 described in this extract from an article in the *Observer*[15] highlights forces that shifted the D curve to the right (D$_1$ to D$_2$) and the supply curve to the left (S1 to S2), a process that inevitably resulted in higher prices (OP2).

1973 also saw spectacular rises in the price of copper and an analysis of this situation reveals the following forces at work:

(a) Speculative purchase of copper to 'hedge' against uncertainty in the world money market. The uncertainty of world money particularly the £ and $ has led people and institutions to hold their assets in the form of commodities.

(b) This action in (a) has led users of copper to purchase more than normal and build up stocks for fear of further price rises.

(c) The Rhodesian/Zambian border dispute brought all kinds of problems on the supply side. Nearly half of Zambian copper shipments previously went out via Rhodesian Railways to the port of Beira in Mozambique. Now these are having to go out via alternative routes that are not yet geared up for the extra traffic. Imports of materials used by the copper mines have also been affected. The net result must inevitably be a short-fall in deliveries from Zambia.

(d) The Chilean mines are suffering from the aftermath of the nationalization of the previously U.S. owned mines, which resulted in a serious loss of experienced technical staff and of facilities for servicing and acquiring spare parts for existing American mining machinery. Output recovery has been hampered further by the counter-revolution which took place in the autumn of 1973.

26. Conclusion

Enough has been said in this chapter to demonstrate that pricing is a very complicated subject involving considerations far beyond that stated in economic theory. There is no formula for fixing prices and there are no easy short cuts. Understanding the logic of incremental analysis is vital to correct decision making.

Marginal cost pricing is now becoming more popular in Great

Britain. Increased international competition and entry into the Common Market with the eventual removal of all barriers to trade is making firms rethink their pricing policies with the result that flexibility while remaining profitable is receiving increasing attention.

To conclude this chapter and to impress upon the student the importance of the approach outlined above, let us consider the following example. Two firms, A and B, produce similar products with identical equipment and efficiencies. The maximum price that can be charged in the market is a combination of (i) the willingness of the consumer to pay and (ii) competition between the suppliers. The two firms have identical cost structures but A pursues an incremental approach while B still uses full cost.

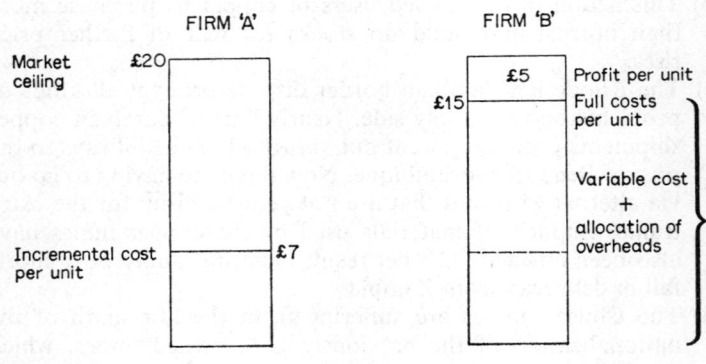

FIG XXI

In Figure XXI it can be seen that A knows it can be flexible yet still profitable, between £7 and £20. It will continue to earn a positive contribution to its overheads for every price that exceeds £7. Its competitive ability is enhanced by this knowledge.

Firm B on the other hand would consider the small range £15 – £20 as being the extent of its flexibility and any other firm offering the product at any price below £15 would continually out-compete Firm B.

REFERENCES

1. Alfred R. Oxenfeldt, *Pricing for Marketing Executives*, Belmont California: Wordsworth Publishing, 1961.
2. H. Speight, *Economics and Industrial Efficiency*, Macmillan, 1969, Chapter 9.
3. Recent research by Prais shows that the top 100 firms contribute 55 per cent of industrial output.
4. James S. Early, 'Marginal Policies of "Excellently Managed" Companies', *A.E.R.*, 1956.
5. A. D. Kaplan, J. B. Dirlam and R. F. Lanzillotti, *Pricing in Big Business*, Brookings Institution (U.S.A.).
6. W. W. Haynes, *Managerial Economics: Analysis and Costs*, Business Publications, 1969.
7. Bergfield, James S. Early and Knoblock, *Pricing for Profit and Growth*, McGraw Hill, 1957.
8. James S. Early, op. cit.
   Kaplan, Dirlam and Lanzillotti, op. cit.
   In addition the work of Hall and Hitch, 'Price Theory and Business Behaviour', *O.E.P.*
   W. W. Haynes, *Pricing Decisions in Small Business*.
9. John Sizer, *An Insight into Management Accountancy*, Pelican, 1969, Chapter 9;
   and 'The Accountants Contribution to the Pricing Decision', *Journal of Management Studies*, May 1966, pp. 129–50.
10. H. Speight, op. cit., p. 229, Chapter 9.
11. Joel Dean, *Managerial Economics*, Prentice Hall, 1951.
12. Kotler, *Marketing Management Planning Analysis and Control*, Prentice Hall, 1972.
13. P. O. Steiner, 'Peak Load and Efficient Pricing', *Q.J.E.*, November 1957, pp. 585–610.
    J. Hirschleifer, 'Comment', *Q.J.E.*, November 1957, pp. 451–62.
14. J. Hirschleifer, 'On the Economics of Transfer Pricing', *Journal of Business*, July 1956, pp. 172–84 and 'Economics of the Divisionalized Firm', *Journal of Business*, April 1957, pp. 96–108.
    David Solomons, *Divisional performance: Measurement and Control*, Financial Executives Research Foundation, 1965.
15. *Observer*, 12 August 1973, 'Grain Crisis Out of Control', Lawrence Marks.

PROGRESS TEST

1. Can traditional economic theory be applied to pricing problems in practice or do serious limitations exist that make its application impossible? (1)
2. What do we mean by full cost pricing and can this method of pricing entirely take the place of pricing by traditional economic theory? (2, 3, 4, 5)
3. What is the difference between incremental and marginal cost pricing? (8, 9, 10, 11)
4. *Firm XYZ Ltd.*

Product	A	B	C	D
Selling Price	10	12	8	9
Direct Labour	1·50	2·00	1·75	2·00
Direct Material	2·50	2·00	2·25	2·00
Material Spoilage	0·50	1·00	0·25	1·00
Departmental Expenses				
Direct	1·00	1·50	1·25	1·50
Indirect	2·00	2·50	1·50	1·50
	—	—	—	—
Factory Cost	7·50	9·00	7·00	8.00
Selling and Administration Expenses	1·50	1·00	1·00	1·50
	—	—	—	—
Total Cost	9·00	10·00	8·00	9·50

What is the marginal cost of the four products A, B, C and D in the above table? Would firm XYZ Ltd. increase its profitability by ceasing to produce products C and D? (3 and 12)

5. Given the figures below what percentage mark up on cost should the firm employ to achieve a rate of return of 20 per cent? (4)

   Variable Cost   £8 per unit
   Fixed Cost   £1,500,000
   Normal Production   75,000 units
   Normal Capital Employed: Variable   £15 per unit
                                           Fixed   £3,000,000

6. Why can a firm pursue a much more competitive policy when its pricing is based on Incremental and Marginal Cost principles rather than full cost principles? (26)

6 THE PRICING OF NEW PRODUCTS

1. Introduction

A product may be called new for two reasons:

(a) because it is a novelty in the fullest sense of the word and is new to the firm and the market as a whole;
(b) it is a new brand, new to a particular firm, but representing a product which is well known to the market.

Very often practice has shown that pricing a new brand can present more problems than pricing an entirely new product. The reason for this is that although information might be available to guide a firm in its price decision, its own brand has to fit into an established pattern of prices and quality expectations of the consumers.

Many of the factors to be taken into consideration are common to pricing a new brand or a new product.

2. New products

New products require a special treatment because they are distinctive; no one else sells quite the same thing. This distinctiveness, however, is only temporary and the speed with which your product loses its uniqueness depends on a number of factors:

(a) Total sales potential.
(b) The investment required for rivals to manufacture and distribute the product.
(c) The strength of patent protection.
(d) The alertness and power of competitors.

Although this process of competitive imitation is almost inevitable, the company that introduces the new product can use price as a means of slowing the speed of competitive imitation. The difficulty lies in finding 'the right price' because past experience is no sure guide as to how the market will react to any given price, and because competing products are usually significantly different in nature or quality.

In setting a price on a new product the firm will want to have three objectives in mind:

(a) Getting the product accepted.
(b) Maintaining the market in the face of growing competition.
(c) Producing profits.

Your pricing policy cannot be said to be successful unless you can achieve all three of these objectives.[1]

3. Factors to be considered in fixing a launching price
The first stage in the establishment of the launching price of a new product will be an amalgam of the following considerations:

(a) Company costs incurred in creating, developing, producing and marketing the product. The way to estimate costs is to calculate what the total costs would be with and without the new product; the difference should be assigned to the new product. Allocations of overheads you are already incurring should not be assigned to the new product because they will be the same whether or not you go ahead with the addition to your product line. There is great difficulty in arriving at the 'true' costs for the company in relation to new products. Apart from the manufacturing costs which can be assessed with some accuracy (although problems exist here especially if new processes and materials are being used) the expenditure on product evolution (R. and D.) can often be obscure. Considerable money must be expended in the initial phase of the product launch to give it sufficient impact on the market. Further, money is needed to evaluate continuously the product's performance for the purpose of improvement enabling it to hold and to expand its share of the market, and also to provide a fund for the evolution of both second generation products and other new product concepts.

All pertinent costs must be included if an accurate picture of the true cost generated by the new product is to be obtained by the firm.

(b) The consumers' conception of product utility (this includes estimating market demand).

Price has a double meaning to the consumer:

   i. Its cost to him, i.e. opportunity cost/sacrifice.
   ii. An indication of its intrinsic worth – quality.

It has been proved through controlled experiments that consumers do to a large extent judge quality through price and marketing textbooks are full of examples of products whose demand increased when price was raised and products whose demand fell when price was reduced.

For example, Granger and Gabor[2] quote the examples of fountain pen ink and car wax whose products met with strong consumer resistance at their initial low prices but whose demand increased when price was increased.

(c) The reactions of competition to a new product in an established market or by all manufacturers to a new product concept.

All products must be considered as potential competitors to a new product as they are all struggling to achieve priority placing in the consumers' purchasing budget. The degree of competitive power between direct and near competitors will depend upon the classification of these products in relation to the new product.

4. Competitive products

These may be categorized under three main headings[3]:

(a) Direct competitors – products which offer a direct substitution within the consumers' concept of that particular type of product's utility.
(b) Near competitors – products which fulfil a part but not the whole of the consumers' concept of that particular type of product's utility.
(c) Indirect competitors – all other products which are vying for a share of the consumers' discretionary purchasing power.

The introduction of a new brand would draw reaction from the three categories listed above but a new product concept would only receive competition from categories (b) and (c).

Competitive reactions must be carefully considered. Competition may increase promotional activity on existing products in an effort to reduce the impact of the new product on the consumer. Prices may be reduced in the market place in an attempt to maintain existing market shares and also any factor within the total marketing mix (price, quality, quantity, design, packaging, flavour, colour, size, etc.) can be varied and used as offensive weapons to fight market intrusion.

(d) The economic situation and future trends. The economic situation in the overall market as well as that within the specific market must be thoroughly and continuously evaluated. Government policy with relation to taxation, changes in H.P. terms, lowering or raising of tariff barriers, general political climate can all affect the demand for a product, and directly affect the variability of the product in the market place. A firm can produce a new product whose design is right, which performs a useful function and is well priced from the consumer point of view but if it is launched at the wrong time (in the case of consumer durables, say, when there is a restriction on credit and H.P. regulations have been tightened) it will fail to make an impact on the market.

(e) The influence of what the company requires a product to achieve in subjective terms of image and prestige as well as the objective terms of contribution to company profitability (see Chapter 1 on company objectives).

The above five points provide information that will tend to show if the product is a feasible proposition in the market place in measurable terms – profit. They will also indicate a hypothetical range of prices which may be changed, but do not specify the exact price to be adopted. The exact price may be a policy decision in line with the marketing strategy employed in launching the new product.

5. Competitive strategies

Keeping the above objectives and factors in mind (2, 3 and 4) a firm can choose to implement two strategies.

1. Skimming pricing. Achieving the maximum contribution to profit in the shortest possible time by charging the highest possible price that the market will bear.

2. Penetration pricing. Achieving the maximum market penetration by charging a low price to create large volume sales.

There are a number of intermediate positions but the issues are made clearer by examining the two extremes.

6. Skimming policy

For products that represent a drastic departure from accepted ways of performing a service or filling a demand, a strategy of high prices coupled with large promotional expenditures in the early stages of market development has frequently proved successful. Skimming pricing is likely to be successful under the following conditions:

(a) Where the life cycle of the product is expected to be short – a feature of markets with a high rate of innovation incidence, e.g. fashion.
(b) With new product concepts where the buyer has no measuring rod for comparisons of value and utility.
(c) Where sales seem relatively inelastic to price, but responsive to information promotion.
(d) Where one can take the cream of the market at a high price before attempting to penetrate the more price-sensitive areas of the market. This means one can get more money from those who do not care how much they pay, while building up experience to fill the mass market with lower prices.
(e) It is a way of feeling out demand. It is frequently easier to start out with a high 'refusal' price and later reduce the price, when the facts relating to demand become known, than to set a low price initially and then boost the price to cover unforeseen costs.
(f) It provides a fund for financing the product through its costly initial phases of introduction.
(g) Future product modifications and improvements to meet changing consumer concepts of utility can be incorporated without price changes.
(h) The company may have limited manufacturing facilities to produce the product or a small sales force to promote the product; therefore, a small but highly profitable segment of the market in the premium area may be the most economic for the company to operate.

7. Penetration policy

A skimming price policy is not always the answer because high initial prices may prevent the development of a consumer loyalty with many buyers upon whom one will be eventually relying to provide a mass market. By creating a need for the product but preventing the mass of consumers from purchasing because of a high initial price one is setting up a 'captive market' for a competitor who wants to enter at a lower price. Penetration pricing is likely to be desirable under the following conditions:

(a) Where a high degree of price elasticity exists even in the early stages of introduction.

(b) Where high volume sales will tend to give economies of large scale production (bulk material purchase, higher plant utilization, distribution, rationalization, etc.).

(c) Where the product is faced with threats of strong potential competition very soon after introduction. Such a policy tends to discourage competitive entry into the market as short to medium-term profits will appear to be low if a high level of investment is required in plant, labour, and other production facilities.

(d) Where there is no 'élite' market, that is a body of buyers who are willing to pay a much higher price in order to obtain the latest and best.

(e) In certain conditions a low price may penetrate an important section of the market not yet tapped by existing high-priced products.

It is the speed with which competitors react and attempt to bring out a substitute that is really the prime factor to be taken into consideration when deciding on a policy of skimming or penetration. A skimming strategy can be turned into a penetration strategy at any stage in a product's life-cycle, but a close watch must constantly be kept on one's competitors because a high initial price might have spurred one into making some initial investment with the intention of competing. The fact that one has lowered the price might not deter him from continuing to produce a competitive product and attempting to take some of the market. (This, of course, depends on how far he has progressed with his expenditure and the time period required for him to compete effectively. See Chapter 4 for the importance of the time factor.)

8. The 'right' price

In addition to the above factors Clive Granger and André Gabor[4] have developed a technique to aid in the pricing of new brands. Their research is based on the idea that a 'right price'[5] exists and that ideally the price of a new brand should be right from the word go, in the sense that at least the great majority of potential customers who favour it should not consider it either too expensive or too cheap. They point out that the price being right does not guarantee success if the product is of poor quality but that 'it is an accepted fact, we think, that if the price is not right this can be responsible for the failure to capture the market.'[6]

They believe that in setting a price on a new product obtaining information pertaining to:

(a) range of existing prices
(b) share of market of existing brands

is not sufficient because this information only reveals the existing

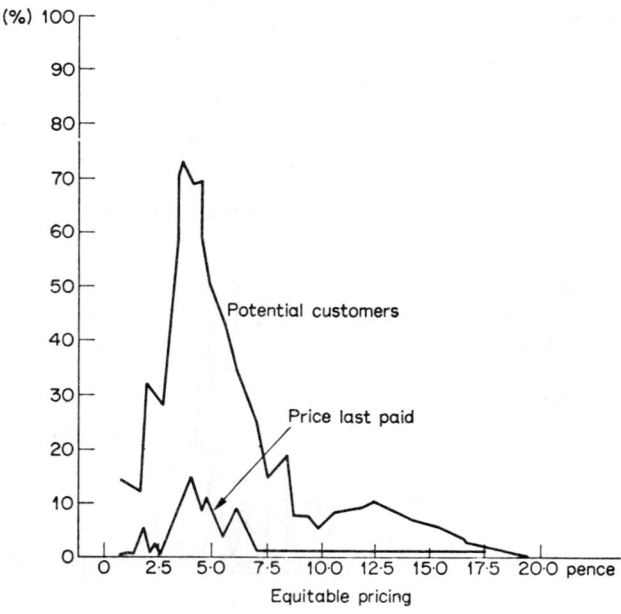

FIG XXII

101

situation rather than the potentialities of the market. Research is required to reveal the attitude of consumers to existing prices. Questions need to be designed so that the following information is obtained:

(a) range of prices considered acceptable by consumers.
(b) share of market of existing brands.
(c) price last paid by consumers.
(d) brands last bought by consumers.
(e) is the customer a regular user? – if not, why not? are the reasons connected with price or quality?

Information gathered in this way will indicate at what prices the greatest source of potential customers lie.

The relationship of price last paid and the schedule of potential customers can indicate the extent to which consumers are satisfied with the existing price structure. This is illustrated in Figures XXII

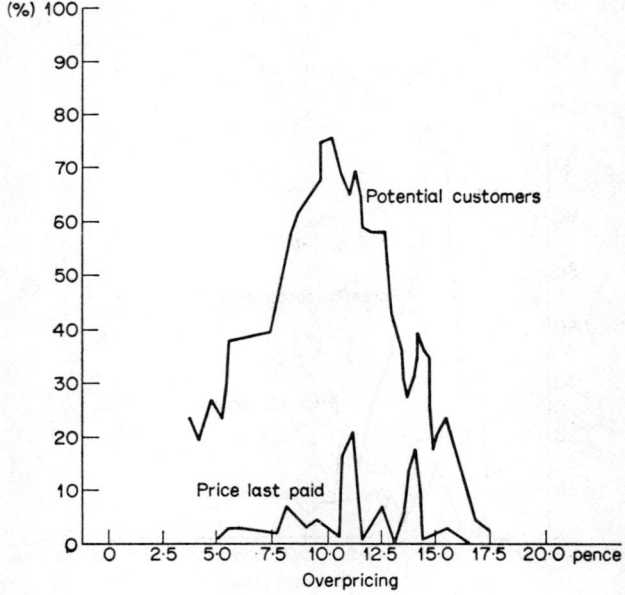

FIG XXIII

and XXIII, which are based on research carried out by Granger and Gabor.[7]

The two figures relate to two well-known household articles and contain the curve of potential customers together with price last paid distribution.

In Figure XXII the relative position of the two curves implies that the structure and general level of prices is one which is considered equitable by the group as a whole, whereas in Figure XXIII they suggest that very substantial proportions of the users regarded the commodity over-priced. The fact that prices to the right of the peak of the curve of potential customers accounted for well over half the purchases signifies that at the time of the inquiry the less expensive brands could not fill the gap, either because they dissatisfied the customers in quality or image terms or because they were not available in a high proportion of retail outlets.

9. Conclusion

All the above factors should be looked at in setting a price. Estimating these factors shrewdly and objectively requires specialized training and experience. Pricing cannot be established by formula; combining the above factors which include accounting, financial and behavioural information requires experience and knowledge of the particular market place.

'You will want to make sure that the pricing analysis is guided by sound principles and that the activities of your specialists are all geared towards the same end – devising a sound, effective marketing and promotional programme in conjunction with a price that will meet your objectives of market acceptance, competitive strength and profits.'[8]

REFERENCES

1. Joel Dean, *Managerial Economics*, Prentice-Hall, 1951, Chapter 8.
2. Clive Granger and André Gabor, 'The Pricing of New Products', *Scientific Business*, August 1965, pp. 141–50.
3. Borne James, 'A Contemporary Approach to New Product Pricing', *Journal of Marketing*, 1968.
4. Granger and Gabor, op. cit.
5. The idea of a right price for every product is deeply rooted in

our psychological make-up. This might not mean one specific price, but a range of price that the consumer considers 'right' in terms of quality and purpose. The range varies from product to product and one must be certain to set a price within this range. At a price below the range people start to question the product's quality and at a price above the range they consider the relationship between satisfaction and sacrifice as being out of balance.

6. Granger and Gabor, op. cit.
7. Granger and Gabor, op. cit.
8. Joel Dean, 'Pricing a New Product', *Financial Executive*, April 1955, pp. 163–5.

PROGRESS TEST

1. What costs must be taken into consideration in setting the price of a new product? (3a)
2. When would a skimming policy be advantageous to a firm? (6)
3. What pricing policy do you think has been adopted in the launching of the following products?

      Biro pens   Electric lawn mowers
      Colour televisions   Touring caravans
      Jaguar XJ12s   Holiday package tours
      Frozen foods

4. What is meant by the 'right' price? (8)
5. When is a product a new product? (1, 2)
6. Certain conditions must exist to make a penetration pricing policy successful. Describe what these conditions are. (7)

7 THE NATIONALIZED INDUSTRIES

1. The background to public enterprise

Up to the beginning of the twentieth century Britain was predominantly a private enterprise economy. The only significant exceptions were the local authorities, the gas and electricity supply industries, and the Post Office.

In the 1920s and '30s this small public sector was extended by the creation of public corporations to deal with specific problems in certain industries, e.g. the Central Electricity Board (1926), the B.B.C. (1927) and the London Passenger Transport Board (1933). However, these were still very small organizations in terms of numbers employed.

The greatest single change in the structure of British industry since the war has been the growth of public ownership. It was not until the series of Nationalization Acts introduced by the Labour Government of 1945-50, that a significant section of industry passed into public ownership.

An important point to note here is that nationalization involves public ownership, but not all publicly owned organizations are nationalized in that many are run by local or municipal authorities. Similarly, whereas the public corporation is the organization form used by the nationalized industries, not all the public corporations involve nationalization, e.g. the Independent Television Authority and the Arts Council are public corporations but they are not nationalized industries. It is our intention in this chapter to concentrate on the operation of nationalized industries.

2. Nationalization in Britain since 1945

The initial surge towards nationalization came in the period of the Labour Government from 1945-50. The nationalization of coal mining, gas and electricity supply, railways, transport and the major airways constituted a significant increase in public ownership, the essential character of which has never been changed. The nationalized industries now employ about 7 per cent of the working population and supply nearly a quarter of gross domestic fixed capital formation in Britain.

When the Conservatives came back to power in 1951, they made some relatively modest changes involving denationalization of the steel industry (with the exception of Richard Thomas & Baldwin) and partial denationalization of long distance road haulage. Nevertheless, in the main, the Conservative Governments of 1951-64 acknowledged the fact of public ownership.

When the Labour Party came back to power in the period 1964-70, they proceeded to nationalize steel once more. Also, the Post Office was changed from being a Government Department to become a nationalized industry.

On returning to office in 1970 the Conservative Government proceeded to become involved in a policy of what has been termed 'disengagement' or 'hiving off'. However, their policy of a return to the market place and a selling off of all the profitable sections of the nationalized industries was in practice a lot more modest than they intended and circumstances forced them to nationalize Rolls-Royce.

Meanwhile, the current Labour Government have promised to introduce nationalization plans which could be almost as sweeping as those undertaken in the 1945-50 era. Ideologically, on the principle of nationalization, the two major parties have never been so far apart.

3. The economic rationale for nationalization

Although most of the protagonists in the nationalization debate were motivated by deep-seated political and ideological objectives, the major argument in favour of nationalization of a particular industry was usually put in economic terms. The following are some of the major economic arguments in favour of nationalization:

(a) The economies of scale argument, i.e. the belief that technical economies of scale could only be achieved by integration and central co-ordination of the public utilities.

(b) The wasteful competition argument, i.e. the idea that any duplication of facilities in industries which were large users of capital would mean that large amounts of fixed capital would be under-utilized.

(c) The run down of fixed investment in some of the basic industries during the war; e.g. the railways, electricity, and the coal industry, needed large amounts of new investment after the war in order to make them competitive. It was argued that private enterprise would not be able to supply the large amounts of capital required.

(d) The social service argument. The commitment to full employment after the war meant that regional unemployment in, for example, coal-mining areas could not be left to the free play of market forces. Also, the provision of uneconomic railway lines might be justifiable on social grounds.

(e) The consideration of the public interest. It was argued that the fortunes of the strategic energy and transport industries were far too important to leave to private control.

(f) It was argued that bad industrial relations in the coal industry had a detrimental effect on the behaviour of the remainder of the labour force.

4. The ideological rationale for nationalization

Although the economic considerations were the major argument put forward at the time of nationalization, the contrasting outlooks of the Conservative and Labour Parties suggest that it would be foolish to pretend that political considerations were unimportant. The major ideological considerations in favour of nationalization were as follows:

(a) The argument that control of the 'commanding heights' of the economy is necessary for effective government planning and control. The basic character of the nationalized industries, engaged in the provision of fuel, power and transport, which are essential requirements for all other industries, bestows upon them a strategic importance. Hence the basic industries were nationalized because their control was fundamental to any effective economic planning.

(b) The argument that nationalization would bring about a better distribution of income. It could, of course, be argued that this could be better achieved by means other than nationalization. Nevertheless, it was hoped that public ownership of the means of production and the gradual elimination of private property would go some way to meeting this objective.

(c) The social benefit argument. It was generally acknowledged that private enterprise was more concerned with private costs and benefits rather than social costs and benefits, and it was hoped that nationalization would enable these social considerations to become an important part of the operation of the industries.

5. The organization of the nationalized industries

The organization of the nationalized industries in Britain is concerned with two major considerations. The first is the legal form of organization which in Britain is the public corporation. The second is whether the industries should be centralized or decentralized.

(a) *The public corporation*

The public corporation is the form of organization that has been adopted for the nationalized industries in Britain. The purpose of the public corporation is to provide an effective combination of business management with public accountability and control. Each public corporation was to have a governing board appointed whose purpose it was to pursue the business management side of the industry. The board has full authority within the organization. Although the board was to be ultimately controlled by a Minister responsible to Parliament, it was intended that the board should have extensive autonomy especially in matters of day-to-day management. It was hoped that the public corporation would represent a form of public ownership which would not stifle initiative and enterprise in its operation.

The public corporation contains the following features. It is a specific legal form, in that it can trade in its own name, sue and be sued, etc. It is a statutory body with its constitution, powers and duties prescribed by law. It is publicly owned. There is some degree of government control which usually includes the appointment of the corporation's governing board, and there may also be control via statutes which allow influence over policy and financial matters. Nevertheless, the corporation is independent in respect of its actual operations.

(b) *Centralization versus decentralization*

The major practical problem faced by the nationalized industries was the issue concerned with the extent of centralization. It is important to point out in this context that decentralization may be either geographical (i.e. divisions, areas, regions, etc.) or functional (e.g. the separation of generation and distribution in electricity supply).

There are a number of arguments in favour of centralization. In the first place there is the need to make the optimum use of scarce resources. Also, it increases the speed with which new techniques and methods could be adopted throughout the industry. There is also the desirability of imposing national standards: note that the trade unions were particularly keen on national pay awards. Moreover, the existence of public accountability meant that the central authority must have control over all parts of its industry.

Nevertheless, the arguments in favour of decentralization are equally imposing. Decentralization encourages the taking of initiative and responsibility, and provides the opportunity for experimentation with new ideas. It also enables each decentralized unit to adapt more closely to the special circumstances of the locality. Moreover, there is the feeling that centralization will promote bureaucracy and remoteness.

It is not surprising then that, in practice, general principles are of little use here and each industry has its own structure, some being more decentralized than others. (See references 5 and 11 for greater detail on each industry.) The important point is that the organizations should change to meet changing circumstances. As Tivey[1] points out, 'there may be changes in the balance of centralization and decentralization, and they should not be regarded as progressive or retrograde by fixed standards, but in relation to changing needs'.

6. Ministerial control of the nationalized industries

The objective here was to achieve some kind of balance between the desire to protect the public interest and the desire to avoid excessive interference in the industries. Consumers' Councils were set up to protect the consumers, but these have in practice achieved little. Control was expected to be achieved through the appropriate Minister, who would himself be responsible to Parliament.

Each corporation is controlled by a particular Minister, e.g. the Minister of Power controls coal, electricity and gas; the Minister of Transport supervises canals, railways, etc.; and the Minister of Aviation is responsible for the national airlines. The Minister appoints members of the board and also has the power of dismissal. The Minister can give directions of a general character in matters relating to the national interest. Note that in this context almost any interference can be justified as being in the national interest. In addition to these general controls, the Minister may also possess statutory powers in relation to such issues as reorganization, capital development schemes, etc. Much of the interference that takes place is often in the form of an informal consultation between the Minister and the chairman of the board.

There has been much criticism levelled against the practice of ministerial control. In the first place, informal consultation, although it may make for better relations between the Minister and board chairman, has tended to result in the responsibility for particular decisions becoming blurred. Secondly, it has become extremely difficult to distinguish between matters of day-to-day administration and matters of general policy. It would appear that ministerial influence has been excessive. David Coombes[2] comes firmly to the conclusion that the attempts to exercise political control have led to a degree of detailed ministerial interference which must inevitably strangle any real attempt either to maximize service to the customers or to minimize cost to the taxpayers. It would appear that the method of ministerial control via informal consultation is not fulfilling its desired objectives.

7. Public accountability

Parliament can obtain information relating to the nationalized industries in three main ways:

(a) *Debates*
   If there is important new legislation on an industry, it will be debated. Also, any M.P. may initiate a debate on an industry. However, the only regular debates take place when the Mini-

ster presents the annual reports and accounts. Even so, some industries may go for several years without being debated.

(b) *Parliamentary questions*

In order to maintain managerial independence, M.P.s can ask questions only on matters that are the Minister's responsibility, unless the issue can be proved to be of national interest. Once again, the nebulous nature of the term 'national interest' enables M.P.s to ask questions on almost any issue.

(c) *The Select Committee*

The Select Committee on Nationalized Industries is by far the most important instrument of public accountability. It is made up of a small group of M.P.s which reflects the proportion of the parties in the Commons. Its terms of reference are very broad and it can take evidence from anyone. Usually, it examines one industry at a time and submits one or two major reports annually. It submits a clear appraisal of the problems and prospects facing each industry.

In general the performance of the Select Committee on Nationalized Industries, coupled with the annual publication of accounts and reports by each industry, have represented a reasonable degree of public accountability. As Tivey[3] says 'the real strength of the system lies in the fact that reports and accounts are published; and so a great amount of information, statistical and descriptive, is made available to all'.

However, the real drawback from the point of view of public accountability goes back to the problem of informal consultation between the Minister and the board. Since the Minister has been so closely involved in the formation of the policies of the board, he has consequently always been in the position of defending the board in Parliament. This inhibits the degree of public accountability. (See the Parliamentary debate on the 1968 Select Committee on Nationalized Industries.[4])

8. Theoretical issues in pricing

There are three basic alternative pricing policies which are available to the nationalized industries. The first involves pricing to maximize profits, the second involves some variation of average cost pricing, and the third is the principle of marginal cost pricing.

PRICING IN PRACTICE

One of the major factors to bear in mind in recommending a general pricing principle for the nationalized industries is that some of these industries have overhead costs which form a relatively large part and direct costs a relatively small part of total costs. The latter factor has significant implications for a pricing policy based on marginal cost, since such industries are likely to be operating at a level of output at which the marginal cost is below the average cost, and consequently losses will be made.

Figure XXIV below shows a decreasing cost industry with the price/output combinations of the three alternative pricing policies suggested above.

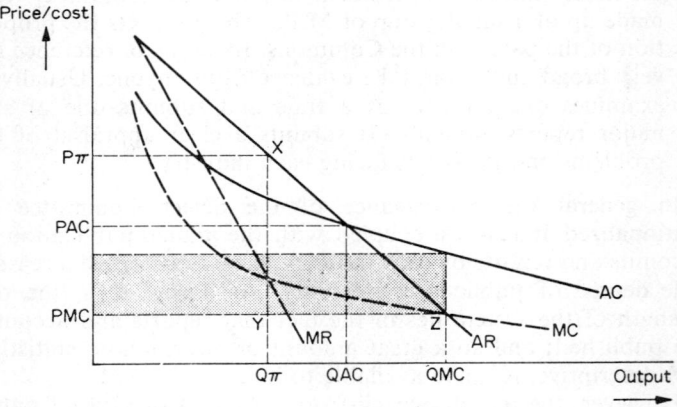

(a) *Profit maximization*

This is the policy indicated in the diagram by the price Pπ and the output Qπ, i.e. the output determination by the intersection of the MC or MR curves. The problem with this pricing policy is that it does not maximize consumer welfare since the consumer will be denied the area of consumer surplus represented by triangle XYZ. The value to the consumer of the additional output (as represented by the price on the demand curve which they would be prepared to pay) exceeds the value of the extra resources used up in the production of the extra output (as represented by the MC curve) since price is greater than marginal cost and consequently a misallocation of resources will result.

A variation on the profit maximization theme is that of charging what the market will bear. However, this type of pricing policy may bring about intense competition which will cause a movement of the demand curve to the left. This may make some of the industry's ventures unprofitable and will result in cross subsidization.

(b) *Average cost pricing*
This type of pricing policy as indicated by the price/output combination PAC/QAC in the diagram does have the advantage of breaking even. This would probably mean an arbitrary allocation of fixed costs among all consumers. Its great disadvantage is that it completely neglects the demand factor. If it were adopted by the railways for example, it would probably mean they would lose much of their traffic to the roads leaving the railways with the same costs to be spread among a smaller volume of output. Moreover, like the profit maximization policy, it too would not represent a welfare optimum since price would be in excess of marginal cost.

(c) *Marginal cost pricing*
This type of pricing policy is indicated in the diagram by the price/output combination PMC/QMC. This pricing principle received most support from the academics who argued that it brought about a welfare optimum and an optimum allocation of resources, e.g. in the case of a bridge once it has been built its opportunity cost is almost zero and the MC of an extra man crossing it is virtually zero, so that if this man is prevented from crossing this bridge because of a positive toll then welfare will not be maximized.

The problem with marginal cost pricing is that in a decreasing cost industry it will result in a deficit as shown by the shaded area in the diagram. Moreover, this deficit is usually financed by the taxpayer. Unless the revenue is raised by a tax on the product of the loss-making enterprise (i.e. make the consumer pay more than MC) then the consumers of the product are being subsidized by the general tax payers. Consequently there will be a redistribution of income in

113

favour of the consumers of the product of the loss-making industry. Conversely, in the case of a surplus.

Moreover, in the case of continual deficits it would be extremely difficult to devise any investment criteria for the industry.

These problems inherent in a short run marginal cost pricing policy led eventually to support for a fourth alternative, namely that of long run marginal cost pricing.

(d) *Long run marginal cost pricing*
Since in the long run one could argue that all costs are variable, then long run marginal cost pricing could be interpreted as covering the indirect as well as the direct costs of a venture. It was hoped that this would both lead us nearer to a welfare optimum, and at the same time enable the adoption of sensible investment criteria since deficits would no longer occur.

However, once again long-run marginal cost pricing tends to neglect the influence of demand. It is unwise to neglect the strength of demand in industries subject to intense competition. For example, it is important to be able to reduce prices to utilize surplus capacity in the short run, or to be able to increase prices to take advantage of monopoly situations.

9. Government guidelines on pricing and investment policy
Government guidelines on pricing and investment policy in the nationalized industries can be split into three distinct phases.

(a) *Pre 1961*
In the initial period of nationalization in the 1940s the major statutory requirement was that they pay their way, taking one year with another which meant that deficits and surpluses would cancel out over a period of time. The costs to be recovered included interest, redemption of capital, depreciation at historic cost and the provision of reserves. They were also required to provide an efficient, economical service to the public.

The very general nature of these guidelines posed a number of problems for the operation of the nationalized industries. The major problems which arose are as follows:

i. The guidelines merely indicated what was to be achieved, not how it was to be achieved, i.e. there were no guidelines on the kind of pricing and investment policies which would achieve the required objectives. Consequently, some of the industries have made a loss and others which have had a surplus are earning a rate of return below the commercial level.

ii. The nationalized industries are enormous users of fixed capital. Therefore, it is essential that this capital be used productively, and produce a viable rate of return. However, the margin between costs and prices have sometimes been very small indeed, partly because of the political and administrative delay that the industries face when trying to raise prices in response to a rise in costs.

iii. Moreover, a low pricing policy encourages excessive demand which in turn requires an even higher level of capital investment to meet this demand. At the same time the low prices depress profits and make the industries more and more dependent on external sources for the financing of their own investment. This in turn placed a heavy burden on the Exchequer and was exacerbated by the fact that at any point in time the financial requirements of the industries may be at odds with the Government's monetary and fiscal policy.

iv. The self-financing investment problem was made worse by the policy of depreciating assets at historic cost rather than replacement costs. As a result the depreciation provisions were inadequate to meet the cost of the replacement capital required.

v. Investment plans were not subject to the 'test of the market', but were determined largely by political decisions. After the war investment was concentrated mainly on the fuel industries of coal and electricity, because of the shortages of fuel, and little consideration was given to the rate of return. In the mid 1950s expansion was sanctioned in the railways and several other industries, but once again little consideration was given to the profitability of these ventures.

The obvious inadequacies of these general guidelines led in

1961 to a White Paper on 'The Financial and Economic Obligations of the Nationalized Industries', which constitutes our phase two.

(b) *The 1961 White Paper*
The 1961 White Paper arose not only because of the inadequacies of the pre-1961 general guidelines, but also because the nationalized industries had not even achieved the limited objectives set by these guidelines. The 1961 White Paper included the following provisions:

  i. That surpluses should cover deficits over a five-year period.
  ii. That provision should be made for depreciation at replacement cost rather than historic cost.
  iii. That an overall rate of return would be negotiated with each industry according to its circumstances, particularly with regard to the extent to which the industry would be required to undertake unprofitable ventures.
  iv. That investment would be allocated according to five-year capital development plans with careful evaluation of low rate of return projects.

The great advantage of the 1961 White Paper was that financial targets were defined in far more precise terms. Nevertheless, it was still deficient in a number of respects:

1. In the first place it made the same basic mistake as the pre-1960 guidelines in that it merely stated the objectives but gave no indication of how these objectives were to be achieved, i.e. there were once again no guidelines on pricing and investment criteria. Consequently, in some instances prices have been based on what the traffic will bear, in other cases on average cost, or on direct cost marked up by a reasonable contribution to overheads, or even the prevailing sense of what was equitable.
2. The investment problem remained as nebulous as ever. Thomson and Hunter[6] question whether 'the economic obligations of these giant, multi-faceted industries could be adequately summed up in a single rate of return?' Moreover, would the rate of return be determined by political rather than economic criteria?

Once again, the inadequacies of these guidelines led to the 1967 White Paper 'Nationalized Industries: A Review of Financial and Economic Objectives'.[7]

(c) *The* 1967 *White Paper*

For the first time in 1967 the Government attempted to lay down guidelines concerning how the desired objectives were to be achieved, particularly in regard to pricing and investment policy. The 1967 White Paper included the following provisions:

  i. The average target rates of return for each industry were still there but they were to be subservient to the application of correct pricing and investment principles, i.e. the nationalized industries were still expected to cover their costs including the provision of replacement capital, but if this financial target conflicted with the application of correct pricing and investment rules, it was more important that the correct pricing and investment rules be applied – 'targets should reflect sound investment and pricing policy, and not vice versa'.[8]

 ii. The basic pricing principle it recommends is that 'prices need to be reasonably related to costs at the margin and to be designed to promote the efficient use of resources within industry'.[9] This is interpreted as long-run marginal cost pricing.

iii. There were to be some exceptions to the general rule – viz. where cross-subsidization may be justified on wider economic or social considerations; where it is impracticable to cost separately minor operations; where the area of unallocatable costs is large; and where innovation may lead to a very rapid reduction in long run marginal cost.

 iv. Loss-making services which were regarded as part of an industry's social obligation were to be separately costed, with the financial responsibility for the provision of such services resting with the Government.

  v. Discounted cash flow techniques became evident in the setting up of a test rate of discount for investment projects which was initially set at 8 per cent but was subsequently elevated to 10 per cent in 1969.

vi. Once again there were to be exceptions to the D.C.F. rate of 10 per cent. It was suggested that in the case of certain major projects that social cost/benefit analysis would be a more appropriate investment appraisal technique.

These represent the current rules which govern the operation of the nationalized industries. They are certainly an impressive step forward in that they attempt to tackle the problem of how desired objectives are to be achieved. The White Paper recognizes that sound investment policy can be built only upon appropriate pricing policies. It is a recognition that price does affect demand and consequently the need for further investment funds. Hence the application of a correct pricing policy is at the crux of the problem of the nationalized industries.

Moreover, it also recognizes that the nationalized industries must as far as possible operate upon commercial principles. The provision of separate finances for the undertaking of unremunerative social services is an admirable support for the operation of discounted cash flow techniques.

Nevertheless, a mere statement of principles, however admirable they may be, does not detract from the sometimes insurmountable problems that appear in the attempt to operate these principles, and it is to these we now turn.

10. Difficulties in implementing the guidelines
There are a number of difficulties that arise in the attempt to implement the principles of the 1967 White Paper.

(a) The cost allocation problem
The 1967 White Paper states that 'the aim of pricing policy should be that the consumer should pay the true costs of providing the goods and services he consumes, in every case where these can be sensibly identified'.[10] The problem is that in many of the nationalized industries it is often very difficult to identify the true costs, e.g. on the railways the marginal cost of an extra man in a carriage is virtually zero unless he happens to be the only person in the carriage, in which case he would have to bear the whole cost of the carriage. Obviously, some averaging will be required here among the passengers on the same train. Moreover, the interconnected-

ness of the whole railway system means that a high proportion of costs are joint costs which must somehow be shared. There is a danger here of too much averaging with insufficient discrimination between traffic flows. Similar problems apply to the other nationalized industries.

(b) *The danger of neglecting demand*

The strict adherence to long-run marginal cost pricing would neglect the utilization of surplus capacity in the short run by reducing prices, and also inhibits the opportunity of taking advantage of excess demand. The nationalized industries have found that expediency dictates that they take advantage of these situations. The pricing of railway passenger traffic for example is based almost entirely on what the market will bear, and there is no pretence that the fares are cost-related. Thus inter-city fares are often higher than suburban and rural services even though costs are lower per passenger mile. The fact is that no one mechanistic pricing system is satisfactory for the nationalized industries or is ever likely to be in the future. The reader is recommended to the works of Thomson and Hunter on the *The Nationalized Transport Industries*[11] and Reid, Allen and Harris on *The Nationalized Fuel Industries*[12] in order to peruse the mountain of complications which have beset each nationalized industry in attempts to apply the principles of the 1967 White Paper.

(c) *Social role of the nationalized industries*

There are two basic issues at stake here.

i. Cross subsidization of unremunerative services. This problem is particularly important in the field of transport and communications where rural areas are heavily subsidized by urban areas. The problem here is that although the cost of servicing these areas differs substantially, the public have come to expect somewhat similar prices for similar services. Although the 1967 White Paper tackled this problem by suggesting that unremunerative social obligations be subsidized by a separate grant from the Government, there is still considerable ambiguity about what does and what does not qualify for such a subsidy. Nevertheless, the White Paper was absolutely right in stating

119

that 'to cross subsidize loss-making services amounts to taxing remunerative services provided by the same undertaking and is as objectionable as subsidizing, from general taxation, services which have no social justification'.[13]

ii. Cross subsidization as an instrument of regional policy, e.g. high cost coal mines have usually been in areas of high unemployment and it has been argued that the social problem of unemployment requires that these high cost mines be subsidized by the profitable ones in other regions. Similarly, there has been pressure whenever new investment is available for expansion to take place in the depressed regions rather than where it may be more profitable.

(d) *The role of nationalized industries in the management of the economy*

One of the major problems in the operation of the nationalized industries is that governments have from time to time made use of them in the general macro-economic management of the economy. Indeed, it has even been argued by some people that this is the primary reason why they were nationalized in the first place. In any case, whatever one's ideological disposition, the nationalized fuel and transport industries represent inputs to many other industries and are an obvious instrument for price control in times of anti-inflation policy, e.g. in 1971 the British Steel Corporation was forced to cut its prepared price increases by 50 per cent even though it was losing money. Similarly, in 1972 the nationalized industries were forced to adhere to the C.B.I.'s voluntary 5 per cent price restraint.

The investment policies of the nationalized industries have been administered in a similar manner, e.g. in 1971 the proposed investment expenditures of the industries were brought forward in an attempt to combat the unemployment problem.

It is little wonder that faced with these problems the nationalized industries have engaged such difficulties in adhering to the principles of the 1967 White Paper.

11. The peak load pricing problem

An additional problem faced by some of the nationalized industries, particularly the electricity and railways, is that of the peak

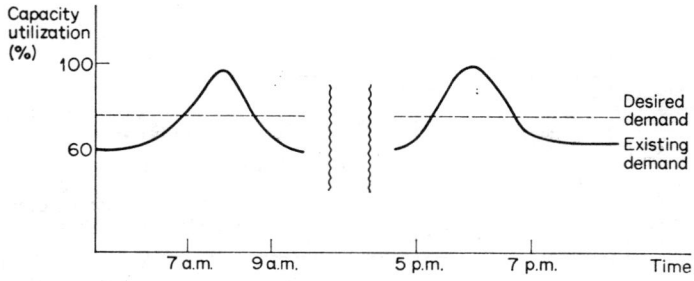

FIG XXV

load problem. The peak load problem has the two basic character-
istics of peaks in consumption from time to time and of difficulties
of storage. This means that extra capacity has to be created to meet
the peak consumption.

The obvious solution to the peak load problem is to charge
higher prices during the peak period in order to damp down the
peak demand and therefore the extra capacity required (which will
be under-utilized during the off-peak period), and in order to make
the high cost users (i.e. the peak users cause the building of the
extra capacity to supply them) pay the full cost of supplying them.

In Figure XXV above it is obvious that capacity is under-utilized
for the major part of the day. Therefore the pricing objective is to
discourage peak demand and to encourage off-peak demand.
If this is achieved, then less capital equipment will be required
to meet the needs of society. One way that has been suggested is to
price off-peak demand at marginal cost, i.e. energy cost, and
to price peak periods at energy cost plus capacity cost.

In practice the problem is complicated by the fact that the peaks
may shift in response to the differential pricing. The prices charged
in this case should be in response to the strength of the peak and
off-peak demands in response to the energy cost, e.g. in Figure
XXVI below the off-peak price is equal to its own energy cost plus
amount CD of its own capacity cost. The peak price covers its
own energy cost plus amount CE of the off-peak capacity cost
plus its own entire capacity cost AE. Capacity is expanded or
contracted until AB = CD. As the peak period demand dampens
down in response to the higher price and as the off-peak demand
increases in response to the lower price, less capacity will be

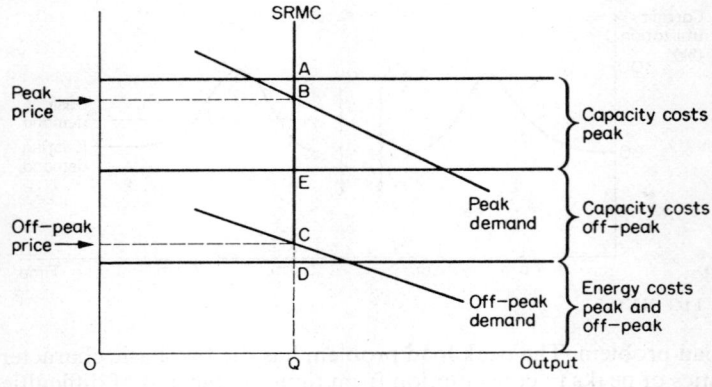

FIG XXVI

required and the demand, and hence price, will be more evenly spread.

British railways and the electricity board have experimented with peak and off-peak pricing. However, once again there are practical problems in their operation. In the first place it is difficult to estimate the price elasticity of demand accurately. There is also the public relations problem of persuading the public to accept differential pricing policies.

12. Performance of the nationalized industries

(a) *The unsuitability of the profit criterion*

The performance of private sector industries is usually judged according to some kind of profitability measure, whether it be total profits earned, earnings per share, the price earnings ratio or some other profit orientated performance measure.

However, it could be argued that it would be inappropriate to apply such a criterion to the nationalized industries for a number of reasons. In the first place, as has been shown above, they are not free to manipulate their pricing and investment policies so as to maximize their profit position. Secondly, they are regarded as industries which should operate in the public interest and this entails not only denying themselves the opportunity to exploit their quasi-monopoly positions, but also imposes upon them the provision of unremunerative burdensome services which are deemed to be required. Finally, the undue political intervention they periodically receive renders profit maximization impossible.

(b) *Other performance measures*

    i. *Labour productivity.* If profitability is rejected as an appraisal technique for nationalized industries then the usual substitute put forward is that of productivity. The most reasoned defence of the nationalized industries has been put forward by Richard Pryke.[14] He argues that throughout the period from 1948 to 1968 the nationalized industries, as a group, have improved their productivity (measured in terms of output per man hour) at a significantly greater rate (3·4 per cent) than general manufacturing (2·8 per cent), which in turn has done considerably better than the private sector as a whole. Moreover, Pryke demonstrates that if we take the more recent period of 1958 to 1968 then the nationalized industries have outperformed private manufacturing by a clear 40 per cent i.e. a labour productivity rate of 5·3 per cent compared with that of 3·7 per cent in private manufacturing.

    Pryke's explanation of this performance is that the nationalized industries are large and unified enough to reap major economies of scale while still, despite the appearance of monopoly, being subject to quite stringent competition (as between gas and electricity, or coal and oil, etc.).

    ii. *Managerial shake-up.* Moreover, Pryke argues that most of the nationalized industries became subject to major managerial shake-ups, of a kind still largely unknown in the private sector, and by and large it has been the most shaken-up who are the most improved. Treasury insistence on the use of more sophisticated management techniques fostered the training and development of managers.

    iii. *Profitable diversification.* The nationalized industries in recent years have shown themselves willing to take on profitable side ventures such as the Coal Board's hotel booking system and the Railway Board's property development schemes. However, there is still considerable ideological debate surrounding this aspect of nationalized industry operation, with the Conservative Party appearing to favour a 'hiving off' of some of these ventures.

13. Conclusion

It would appear that the nationalized industries are here to stay and the only controversy surrounds the extent of nationalization. In this respect the Labour and Conservative Parties have never been so far apart.

In terms of performance the nationalized industries are certainly more efficient than they were. The poor performance in the early years was probably due to the organizational problems at that time, while the improved performance in the 1960s was due to the more sophisticated guidelines the industries were receiving. Hopefully, this improved performance will continue in the future.

REFERENCES

1. L. J. Tivey, *Nationalization in British Industry*, Cape, 1966, Chapter 5.
2. D. Coombes, *State Enterprise – Business or Politics?* Allen and Unwin, 1971.
3. Tivey, op. cit., Chapter 6.
4. *Hansard,* Vol. 777, 1968–9, pp. 1181–1274.
5. Cmnd 1337, H.M.S.O., 1961, 'The Financial and Economic Obligations of the Nationalized Industries'.
6. A. W. J. Thomson and L. C. Hunter, *The Nationalized Transport Industries*, Heinemann, 1973, Chapter 1.
7. Cmnd 3437, H.M.S.O., 1967, 'Nationalized Industries: A Review of Financial and Economic Objectives'.
8. Cmnd 3437, op. cit.
9. Cmnd 3437, op. cit.
10. Cmnd 3437, op. cit.
11. Thomson and Hunter, op. cit.
12. G. R. Reid, K. Allen and D. J. Harris, *The Nationalized Fuel Industries*, Heinemann, 1973.
13. Cmnd 3437, op. cit.
14. R. Pryke, *Public Enterprise in Practice*, McGibbon and Kee, 1971.

PROGRESS TEST

1. What were the major reasons for nationalization in British industry? (3, 4)
2. How were the nationalized industries organized in Britain? (5, 6, 7)
3. Explain and comment upon the principles of 'Ministerial control' and 'Public accountability'. (6, 7)
4. What pricing and investment policies would you recommend for the nationalized industries? (8, 9, 10, 11, 12)
5. Should the nationalized industries be run as commercial organizations? (3, 4, 8, 9, 10, 12)
6. Assess the contributions made by the 1961 and 1967 White Papers on the nationalized industries. (9, 10)
7. Explain the nature of the peak load pricing problem. (11)
8. To what extent should nationalized industries be used as part of the Government's general macro-economic management of the economy? (3, 4, 10)
9. Are the nationalized industries less efficient than private firms? (12)

8 GOVERNMENT INTERVENTION IN THE PRICE MECHANISM

1. Reasons for government intervention

The reasons why governments intervene in the pricing system are many and varied. In the first place the pursuit of their broad economic and social objectives may require interference in the pricing system from time to time. Moreover, the government may regard the allocation of goods and services through particular market structures as needing regulation or sometimes even public ownership. The government may also decide to intervene to attempt to obtain a more equitable distribution of income and to bring about government provision of necessary social services and other quasi-public goods. Similarly, the existence of external diseconomies such as industrial pollution, or of excessive regional inequalities in income and employment, may also be candidates for government intervention.

It is obvious from the above that the reasons for government intervention could be almost endless and it would be impossible in a book of this magnitude to examine all types of government intervention through the price mechanism or indeed government intervention which supersedes the price mechanism. What we intend to do in this chapter is to concentrate on a number of specific issues particularly with regard to pricing and to attempt to make an evaluation of the particular form of government intervention examined. In this respect we have decided to concentrate on four issues, as follows: firstly, the attempt to influence the general level of prices through a prices and incomes policy; secondly, the attempt to fix particular prices below and above the equilibrium price via the use of subsidies, rationing and price support policies; thirdly, the use of indirect taxation as a revenue raising weapon to finance transfer incomes and other government expenditure; finally, the use of monopoly policy in Britain both to contain the growth of adverse market structures and to dis-

126

courage non-competitive behaviour within existing market structures, particularly with regard to pricing.

(a) *Stabilization of the general price level*

Price stability, or more realistically, the slowdown of price level increases, is one of the major economic objectives of the government and ranks alongside other objectives such as full employment, a healthy balance of payments, a high rate of economic growth, etc. The problem with these objectives is that they cannot all be achieved simultaneously, and the objectives themselves often conflict with one another. Professor Phillips[1] has demonstrated the relationship between wage inflation and unemployment via his now famous Phillips curve analysis. As it is not too gross an exaggeration to impute the same relationship between price changes and unemployment, his analysis means that the closer the economy is to achieving full employment the more difficult it becomes to achieve price stability. This is because the pressure of demand is high at high levels of employment whereas supply is not responding to the same extent because of bottlenecks in the economy, shortages of skilled labour, etc. In Figure XXVII below it can be seen that an unemployment level of at least $2\frac{1}{2}$ per cent is needed to ensure some reasonable degree of price

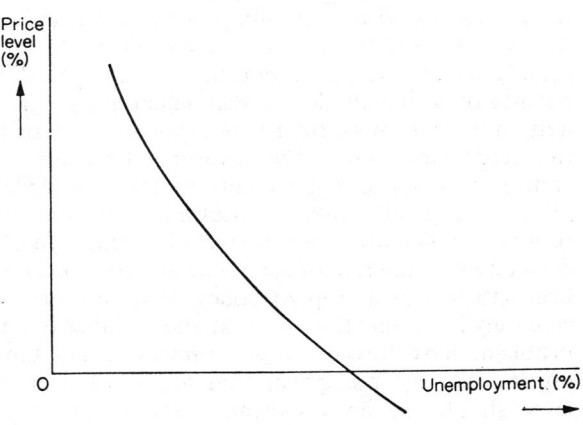

FIG XXVII

stability. While no one would quarrel with the analysis involved it would appear that in recent years the Phillips curve has shifted to the right and a much higher level of unemployment is now required in order to get some sort of price stability. In these circumstances it is not surprising that most governments are more concerned with containing price increases rather than with achieving price stability.

Why then would a government wish to achieve a stable price level? There are two major reasons:

1. In the first place rapidly rising prices are harmful to those people on fixed incomes who are unable to protect themselves against the worst effects of rising prices. A high proportion of the people on fixed incomes are those who rely on transfer earnings (i.e. incomes which are transferred from one section of the community to another via government taxation) such as pensioners. The administrative delay in raising these incomes to keep pace with cost of living increases, leaves this section of the community at the mercy of rising prices.

2. Perhaps a more important issue in recent years (more important to those not on fixed incomes!) has been the effect rising prices have upon the balance of payments. If our prices rise more rapidly than those of the countries we are trading with, then our goods become less competitive with the result that our exports fall (or do not rise as rapidly as imports) and our imports rise, leading to a balance of payments deficit. Britain cannot go on indefinitely importing more than it is exporting and this means that from time to time the government has attempted to rectify the balance of payments problem by deflationary policies designed to take the heat out of the economy, the results of which are a higher level of unemployment and a slow down of the rate of economic growth. This policy has been labelled as a stop-go policy because every time the economy has been allowed to expand, balance of payments problems have forced the government to put the brakes on. It is not surprising then that stabilization of the price level should be an important element of government policy.

The primary instrument the government has used in its attempt to contain the rising general level of prices has been that of a prices and incomes policy which various governments have pursued with differing degrees of enthusiasm at different points in time.

(b) *Individual price fixing to rectify resource misallocation*

Even with the most efficient market structure the government would find it necessary to intervene because of the existence of inequalities in the distribution of income. In practice income is extremely unevenly distributed, and since the price system allocates products according to the strength of monetary demand, this gives the wealthier members of the community an excessive command over resources. The consequences of this maldistribution of income is that resources are diverted from basic necessities to satisfy ostentatious demands made by the wealthier members of the community. Besides taxation, which we will consider in the next section, the government intervenes via the subsidization of basic necessities such as foodstuffs, the use of rationing in cases of extreme shortage, and the introduction of price support policies to maintain the incomes of certain sections of the community such as farmers. Note that even under the recent Conservative administration government subsidies totalled well over £1,000 million, and the Labour government lost no time in its first budget in 1974 in adding £500 million worth of subsidies to food alone.

(c) *Taxation to finance transfer incomes and other government expenditure*

This is related to the income distribution problem mentioned above and also to the need to finance government expenditure. British governments have used both a progressive income tax and high indirect taxation on luxury items to finance transfer incomes such as pensions and family allowances, subsidies, and other public expenditure on socially desirable projects. (We will concentrate on indirect taxation because this has a more direct effect upon the price mechanism.)

(d) *Monopoly policy to contain the development of adverse market structures and non-competitive behaviour*

Chapter 4 has already pointed out the possibility that

non-competitive market structures may lead to resource mis-allocation. The result is that prices may be held higher than in competition due to the existence either of a single firm monopoly or of a policy of collusion among a number of firms.

The major effect that was expected adversely to affect the allocation of resources in non-competitive market structures was the price distortion effect, i.e. the likelihood that prices would be artificially high and hence lead to a reduction in economic welfare. In Figure XXVIII below we have assumed constant cost curves in order to simplify the analysis.

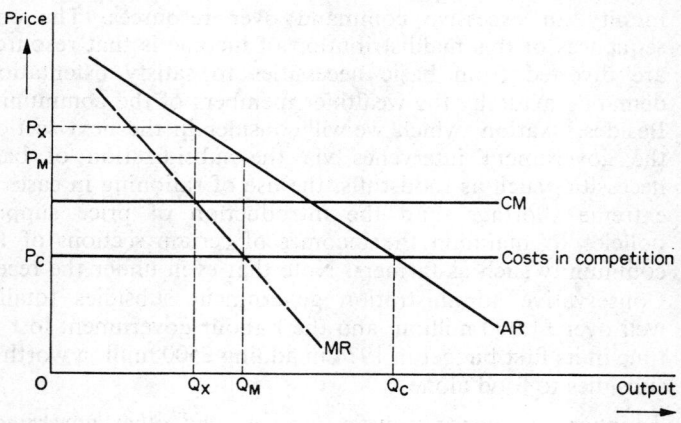

FIG XXVIII

In monopoly, equilibrium will be where MR = MC to give a price of PM and an output of QM. Under perfect competition equilibrium will be where AR = MC to give a price of PC and an output of QC. Thus monopoly leads to a higher price and a lower output than does competition. Moreover, this leads to a reduction in economic welfare since price is above MC (see Chapter 4). However, there are now many economists who argue that the allocative welfare loss which arises from the price distortion effect of monopoly is much less serious than what is called the X inefficiency loss which arises from higher monopoly costs.[2] The argument here is that once market structures have moved away from perfect competition then maximization of profits no longer becomes a condition of survival so that monopolists can allow their costs to rise without disastrous consequences. The result is that both employers and employees can take it easy in large organizations immune from competitive pressures, so that costs are not minimized as in competitive markets. Moreover, it is argued that the welfare loss from X inefficiency is likely to be greater than that from allocative efficiency, because the higher costs from X inefficiency affect all units of output. For example, if in the diagram CM represents the higher monopoly costs caused by X inefficiency then the new profit maximizing price and output would be PX and QX respectively, leading to a further reduction in economic welfare.

Thus, both for reasons of allocative and X inefficiency the government has found it necessary to interfere in the structure of markets. The major instrument of interference has been monopoly legislation.

2. Prices and incomes policies

The commitment of post-war British governments to the objective of maintaining a high level of employment has posed considerable problems for other objectives such as price stability. Due to the great difficulty of achieving these objectives simultaneously, the government has found it necessary to intervene from time to time to check the rise in prices and incomes. It is not intended here to give a historical account of prices and incomes policies in Britain (for such an account see references 3 and 4). Nevertheless, we will examine some of the policy instruments which British governments have used. We will then consider the empirical evidence available to see to what extent such policies have been successful in containing inflation, and finally we will look at some of the problems involved in operating prices and incomes policies.

(a) *Policy instruments*

    1. *General Controls.* These controls are of two broad kinds, namely fiscal and monetary policy. These are not conventionally regarded as being part of a prices and incomes policy, but they are nevertheless the major weapons which the government can use against inflation. The traditional

measures used have been higher interest rates, quantitative and qualitative controls on credit, increases in taxation together with reductions in government spending. These general controls were usually invoked during periods of balance of payments crisis. The problem was that such controls led to checks on investment and output, and an increase in unemployment. It is not surprising then that these general controls were released as soon as the immediate balance of payments danger was over. This policy was known as Stop-Go. This policy operated throughout the fifties and sixties and the most recent example of the brakes being applied was in November 1973 when the Chancellor decided to reduce public spending significantly along with imposing tighter monetary controls. This policy creates unemployment, inhibits economic growth and is generally regarded as undesirable. It is not surprising then that successive British governments have looked for other instruments of control.

2. *Exhortation.* The purpose of this policy is that the government should exhort employers and unions to exercise voluntary restraint in the national interest. The first attempt to influence the rate of inflation with a voluntary policy was in 1948 and there are few British governments since who have not employed this policy at times when there was not a more severe policy in force. It was hoped that such exhortation would not only make the public more conscious of the self-defeating nature of the wage/price spiral, but also that public opinion would be mustered against excessive settlements which obviously paid no attention to the exhortation. The Labour government are committed to a return to voluntary negotiations and hope that their promise of a 'social contract' will be sufficient to contain wage negotiations at a reasonable level. The previous Conservative government also followed a policy of exhortation for a while. For example, in 1971 the Confederation of British Industry agreed to persuade its members not to increase prices if possible or to limit unavoidable increases to 5 per cent over the next year. Similarly, in 1972 the government initiated tripartite talks

with the Trades Union Congress and the Confederation of British Industry in an attempt to obtain a voluntary agreement on policies to restrain prices and incomes. It is noticeable that more severe prices and income controls have only been employed when the milder form of exhortation has proved unacceptable to any of the negotiating parties or is seen to be not working. It remains to be seen how long the Labour government will regard exhortation as being a sufficient restraint.

3. *Guidelines.* With this policy the government not only exhorts but also lays down some criteria such as keeping increases in incomes in line with increases in productivity. The first attempt at such guidelines was in 1957 when the Council on Prices, Productivity and Incomes was set up with the function of keeping under review changes in prices, productivity and incomes. The Trades Union Congress refused to co-operate with the Council. In 1962 the National Incomes Commission was set up to investigate pay claims referred to it by the government, with the recommendation that pay increases should be related to the likely increase in production of 2 to $2\frac{1}{2}$ per cent per annum, subsequently raised to 3 to $3\frac{1}{2}$ per cent. Once again the T.U.C. refused to co-operate and it was not until the Labour government came into office that the government, the employers' organizations and the Trades Union Congress for the first time signed a 'statement of intent' on productivity, prices and incomes. In April 1965 the National Board for Prices and Incomes replaced the National Incomes Commission, its function being to investigate price and wage increases referred to it by the government, the criteria once again being that the annual average rate of increase in money incomes per head be related to the likely productivity growth of 3 to $3\frac{1}{2}$ per cent. This was to be accompanied by an early warning system whereby all proposed price and wage increases were to be notified in advance so that the Board could report and advise before the increase was approved. The Labour government then tried one year of statutory powers (which we will consider shortly), before reverting once again to

the guidelines policy, the suggested norm varying from zero in 1967 to $3\frac{1}{2}$ per cent in 1968, to $2\frac{1}{2}$ per cent to 4 per cent in December 1969. Also the government's power to delay increases varied from 3 months in 1969 to 12 months in 1968 and back again to 3 months in 1969. The Conservative government in 1970 started with a policy of exhortation but in November 1972 found it necessary to introduce statutory controls.

4. *Statutory Controls.* There have only been two periods of statutory controls on prices and incomes in this country. In July 1966 the Labour government introduced a six month general 'standstill' on wages, salaries and prices, to be followed by another six months of 'severe restraint'. The government took statutory powers to enforce the standstill on unions and employers. The only price exceptions during the standstill related to seasonal changes in supply, tax changes, or higher costs of imported raw materials, while incomes exceptions included annual increments and increased output. The only further exceptions allowed during the six month period of severe restraint related to low paid workers and increased productivity. These statutory controls only lasted twelve months. The only other period of statutory controls was that brought in by the Conservative government in November 1972 and which became known as Phase I, and later Phases II and III. This also provided for a complete standstill from the 30 November 1972 to 31 March 1973, so far as incomes were concerned, and 28 April so far as prices were concerned, the extra delay on prices being because of the introduction of Value Added Tax. Once again there were exceptions such as fresh food and imported raw materials so far as prices were concerned, and annual increments so far as incomes were concerned. This was immediately followed by Phase II which set up a Price Commission and a Pay Board to operate the statutory price and pay code respectively. Price increases might be permitted if certain 'allowable' costs had risen (such as fuel or power, rent or rates, interest charges, etc.) or if investment might be jeopardized, but only in so far as the increases do not

lead to excessive profit margins. Income increases were limited to £1 per week plus 4 per cent of the average wage bill for any group of workers, with a maximum of £250 a year for any one individual. In 1973 the statutory controls were again maintained in Phase III but the policy was much more flexible, particularly with regard to incomes. Income increases were to be fixed at 7 per cent plus payment for unsocial hours and a further cost of living increase (40p a week) could be invoked for each 1 per cent that prices rose by more than 7 per cent since October 1973. Phase III then was considerably more flexible than any of the other statutory controls which had existed in Britain.

(b) *Problems of operating a prices and incomes policy*

There are considerable problems in attempting to operate a prices and incomes policy. In the first place it is extremely difficult to get agreement between the government, the unions and the employers as to the cause of inflation. The likelihood is that inflation is caused by a multitude of factors including the demand for labour, trade union pressure, tax changes, import prices, etc., many of which operate simultaneously though with varying degrees of intensity at different points in time. Even if the government, the employers and the unions did agree that cost push was a major contributor, there are still the ominous problems of trying to implement an agreed policy. As Cairncross[5] pointed out, the T.U.C. do not control wages, the C.B.I. does not control prices, and even the response of the economy to government policy itself is subject to international and other domestic influences. It has always been recognized that prices are extremely difficult to control and monitor except among large firms, but wages too are difficult to control because about 40 per cent of workers in manufacturing industry are paid by results with much of the negotiation taking place at plant level, leaving ample opportunity for wage drift.

There is no question that a wage freeze works, at least as far as incomes are concerned, for a short period of time. However, the build up of pressures such as the appearance of anomalies, wage drift, the effect of import prices, etc., means that any freeze inevitably breaks down after about six months. Inevitably, the wage freeze is superseded by a policy of guidelines, either statutory or non-statutory. However, just as inevitably, the problem of relativities comes to the fore; workers in booming industries demand a share in the higher profits, while workers in declining industries maintain that they equally have the right to maintain their relative position *vis à vis* other groups of workers. It is little wonder then that successive British governments have found it extremely difficult to implement successfully a Prices and Incomes Policy.

(c) *The effects of a prices and incomes policy*
It was the 1965-70 Labour government and the 1970-74 Conservative administration who have made the most rigorous attempts to introduce a policy for prices and incomes. Yet during the five years of Labour administration prices and incomes rose faster than in the previous five years, while similarly during the successful Phase II operation (successful in the sense that no one broke it) of the Conservative administration, consumer prices rose 10 per cent in the year and wage rates rose 15 per cent. It would appear then that prices and incomes policies have achieved considerably less than was expected of them.

In so far as the econometric studies are concerned (relating both to the U.S. and the U.K.) the broad conclusion appears to be that the effect of incomes policy on the wages side appears to be about a 1 per cent shift of the Phillips curve to the left, while on the prices side there appears to be little or no direct effect (see Burton[6]). However, more recently Lipsey and Parkin[7] using U.K. data have argued that incomes policy not only shifts the curve to the left (so far as the wage effect is concerned) but alters its slope due to a combination of induced restraint and guidepost following behaviour. Thus in Figure XXIX below the effect of an incomes policy is to pivot the Phillips curve from position AA to position BB. If Lipsey and Parkin are correct, and there is considerable controversy surrounding their findings and the conclusions they draw from them, then the implication is that the effect that incomes policy has on wage inflation depends on the level of unemployment. Thus to the left of point X (which Lipsey and Parkin have estimated

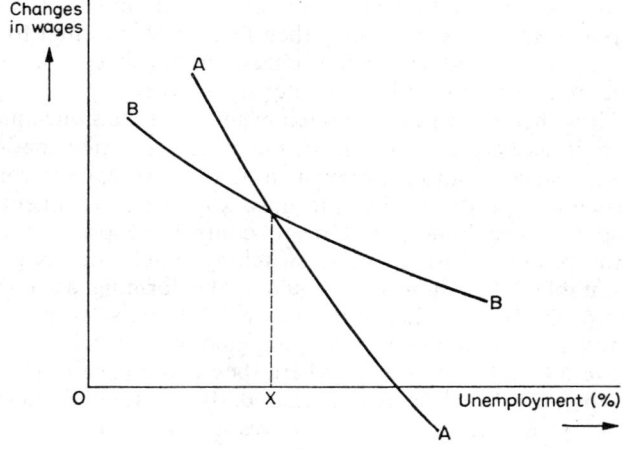

FIG XXIX

to be 1·8 per cent for the U.K.) incomes policy is desirable in that it considerably improves the trade-off between wage inflation and unemployment, whilst to the right of point X incomes policy would be extremely undesirable in that it would considerably worsen the trade-off.

Perhaps the only conclusion to be drawn from all of this is that extreme caution should be used in propagating a prices and incomes policy. Certainly the causes of inflation are complex and are not easily manipulated by any one particular instrument. To quote from Cairncross[8]: 'There is the need to combine it [incomes policy] with policies aimed at regulating the pressure of demand and insulating the economy as far as possible from fluctuations abroad.' Never has this been so true as in the years of the recent Conservative administration.

3. Price fixing of individual products

(a) *Price fixing below the equilibrium price*
It is extremely difficult for a government to fix the price of any particular product because of interdependencies in the pricing system, i.e. because all prices are related to one another. Suppose the government tried to fix the price of milk

137

at a price below that at which $D = S$. If milk is the only product that is fixed in price then farmers will switch to producing other products such as cheese, butter, livestock, crops, etc., and very little milk will enter the market.

How then can the government ensure that the same amount of milk as before comes on to the market, despite the lower price? Since in an economy such as ours we cannot compel farmers to produce milk, the only way the government can stop this switching would be to control the price of other farm products also so that switching would no longer be profitable. This, however, would make farming as a whole less profitable, and hence farmers will be unable to pay competitive rates to maintain capital and labour which would move into other industries where they could earn more. This is obviously not the result desired. It is essential therefore that, unless the government desires a reduction of resources employed in a particular industry, any price control of a particular product must be accompanied by a subsidy.

1. *Subsidies.* The obvious solution to the problem above is to pay the farmers who produce milk a subsidy, so that their total revenue would be the same as if the price of milk was not fixed. It is then necessary to fix the margins added by the retailer so that the price of milk remains unchanged. Note that although the subsidy is paid to the farmer, it is the consumers of milk who are actually receiving the benefit since they are obtaining milk at a price lower than it would have been if it wasn't subsidized.

Note that the 1974 Labour manifesto pledged the Labour government to a policy of subsidizing the major foodstuffs. This was an attempt to protect the community against higher food prices.

Figure xxx below shows how a subsidy can be used. S1 and D represent the supply and demand curves in the absence of a subsidy. If a specific subsidy per unit of output is now given to the product the supply curve will shift downwards to S2 which will be lower than S1 by the amount of the subsidy. The vertical difference between the two supply curves measures the amount of the subsidy and therefore S2 will be parallel to S1.

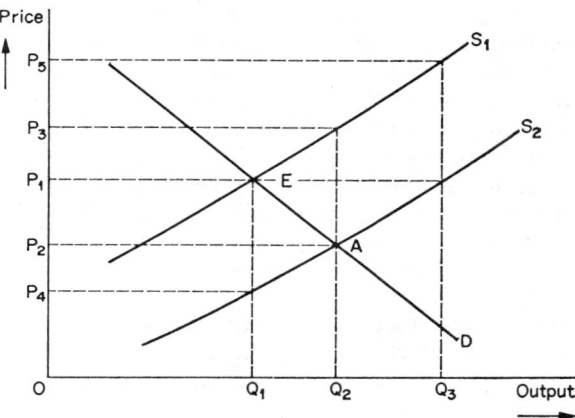

FIG XXX

The new equilibrium point after the subsidy will be A (the original equilibrium was E) where the demand curve cuts the new supply curve. The output of the subsidized product increases from OQ1 to OQ2 and the price paid by consumers falls from P1 to P2. Note, however, that the price received by producers of the product rises from OP1 to OP3. Hence both consumers and producers benefit from the subsidy, the extent of the benefit depending upon the elasticity of the demand and supply curves. The more inelastic the demand curve the lower the price the consumers will have to pay and hence the greater the benefit they receive. This can be seen by rotating the demand curve through the original equilibrium point E. If the demand curve was completely inelastic (i.e. vertical) then the price paid by the consumers would be equal to P4 and the producers would receive the original price P1 with no extension of output. Conversely, if the demand curve were perfectly elastic, the price paid by the consumers would remain at P1 whereas the producers would receive P5 with output expanded to Q3. Similarly, the greater the elasticity of supply the lower the price paid by the consumers. The reader can demonstrate this by using the extreme cases of perfect elasticity and zero elasticity.

139

The problem with subsidies is that they can only be applied to one or two major products such as bread, milk, etc., because such products are consumed in such large quantities that they require an enormous amount of financing. The Healey budget of March 1974 added £500 million to food subsidies, £127 million of which was used to reduce the price of milk by 1p per pint. Milk subsidies now total £272 million. It is also estimated that £21 million is required to avoid a $\frac{1}{2}$p rise in the price of bread. Moreover, subsidies are not selective in that they aid all consumers, rich and poor alike. It could be argued that the tax revenue used for paying subsidies could be better employed directly helping the poor in the form of larger family allowances, supplementary income for low-paid workers, etc.

2. *Rationing.* In cases of extreme shortage of a particular product the government may decide that the price mechanism will not allocate the scarce product efficiently. In such extreme cases rationing may be used. The British government issued ration books for petrol at the end of 1973 because of the Arab oil boycott, although in this case it turned out to be merely a precaution and rationing (except by price) was not introduced. In Figure XXXI below the effect

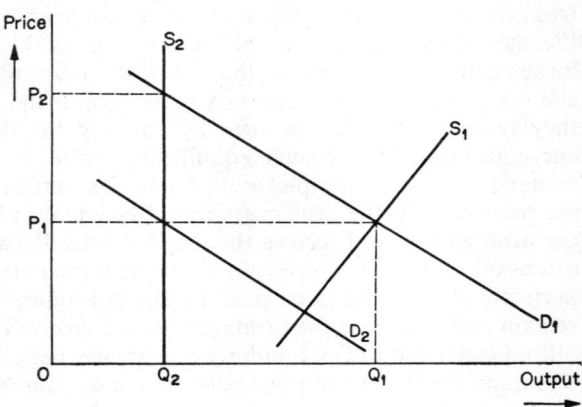

FIG XXXI

of the oil boycott was to shift the supply curve for petrol to the left from S1 to S2. If the price mechanism is allowed to work freely this would force the price up to P2 and output down to Q2. The effect of rationing is to cause a similar shift to the left of the demand curve, preventing or moderating the rise in prices. Thus, the effect of rationing would be to ensure that the relatively poorer consumers of the product would not be priced out of the market by the extortionate prices that wealthier consumers of the product would be prepared to pay. In the event the British government decided to let the price mechanism do the rationing.

Rationing, however, permits no freedom of choice (other than not to consume) so that consumers are no longer able to optimize their expenditure patterns in that consumers who value the product very highly get no more than consumers who have little use for it. Moreover, there are also the cost of resources used up in administering the system and preventing a Black Market forming. But, most important of all, by preventing a shortage leading to a higher price, rationing inhibits the generation of profits necessary to bring forth new sources of supply. Thus rationing is advisable only in extreme circumstances.

(b) *Price fixing above the equilibrium price*

A typical example of governments wanting to raise the price of particular products above the equilibrium price is that of the agricultural price support policies employed by many countries, the main objective of which is to enable farmers to receive greater incomes than would otherwise be the case. There are a number of ways of achieving this. In Figure XXXII below OP1 and OQ1 are the equilibrium price and output in the market place.

Suppose the government was to guarantee the farmers a price of OP2, then the farmers would want to produce OQ2 while the consumers would only wish to purchase OQ3. Thus, in order to maintain the guaranteed price OP2 the government would be forced to buy up the surplus Q3–Q2 which it could then stockpile for future use if the good is durable.

However, a more likely situation is that the government would make sure that this excess supply did not arise by

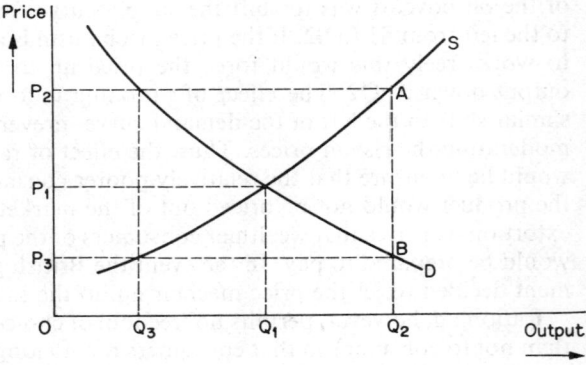

FIG XXXII

controlling the amount of output produced at level OQ3. Restrictions on imports may be used when imports form an appreciable proportion of the total supply. The U.S. Government guarantees the price of agricultural products by combining both these policies of purchasing excess supplies and at the same time imposing quantitative controls on output. The Common Market uses variable import duties to restrict imports to a level which when combined with domestic output, produces just sufficient output to meet the demand at the support prices.

Note that the U.K. Government uses the alternative policy of paying deficiency payments (i.e. subsidies) to farmers which give the farmers higher prices than the consumer pays. In order to ensure that the farmers get the guaranteed price OP2, the government have to pay the farmers a subsidy of AB per unit since the consumers would only be willing to pay OP3 for an output of OQ2. This is partly why food prices were generally lower in the U.K. than in the Common Market prior to British entry.

4. Indirect taxation and the price mechanism

Indirect taxation may be placed upon a product either for revenue raising reasons or to discourage its consumption. The revenue raised by this means may be used by the government for public expenditure to finance transfer incomes such as pensions, etc., or for any other objective of its economic policy. For example, the 1974 Labour budget (March) required the government to raise an extra £1,240 million per annum to finance the increase in pensions granted. Thus, governments have found it necessary to intervene in the pricing mechanism for revenue raising reasons.

An indirect tax may either be a specific tax (i.e. a specific amount per unit of a good) or an *ad valorem* tax (i.e. a given percentage of the price of the good).

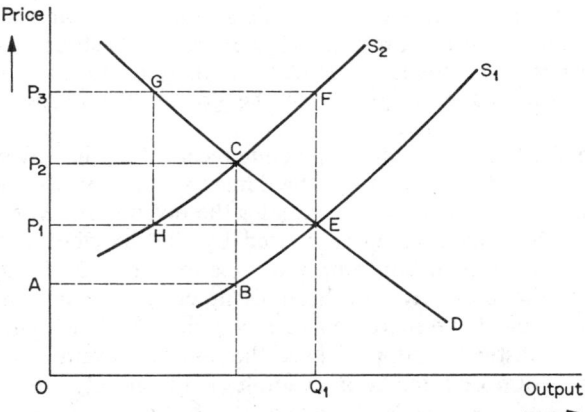

FIG XXXIII

In Figure XXXIII above P1 and Q1 are the equilibrium price and output before the tax is imposed, as determined by the intersection of the original supply curve S1 and the demand curve D. The imposition of a specific tax will raise the supply curve to S2 where S2 is vertically higher than S1 by the amount of the tax. In the case of a specific tax the supply curves will be parallel because the amount of tax per unit of output is the same whatever the price. If the tax was an *ad valorem* tax the supply curves would move further apart as they move to the right because the amount of the tax is higher the higher the price. In the diagram we have assumed a specific tax.

The new equilibrium price and output will be at P2 Q2 where the demand curve cuts S2. The total tax revenue raised is rectangle

143

P2 CBA (i.e. a tax of CB per unit multiplied by the output OQ2). However, the price paid by the consumer has not risen by the full amount of the tax, since the new price is OP2 whereas if the whole tax had been passed on to the consumer the price would have been OP3. Thus the producers themselves have borne part of the tax. To what extent the tax will be passed on to the consumer will depend upon the elasticity of the demand and supply curves. Once again, the effect can be demonstrated by rotating the demand curve through the original equilibrium point E. As can be seen, the more inelastic the demand curve the greater the proportion of the tax borne by the consumer. This confirms what we would expect since if firms can pass on the tax to consumers without losing sales, then this is what they are likely to do. Similarly the more elastic is the supply curve the greater the burden of tax borne by the consumer.

Note also that the total tax revenue received by the government depends upon the elasticity of the demand and supply curve. The more inelastic the demand the greater the revenue raised from the tax since the increased price caused by the tax does not bring forth a reduction in consumption. For example, if the demand curve in the diagram had been completely inelastic then tax revenue would have increased to rectangle P3 FE P1. Similarly, the more elastic the supply curve the less tax revenue raised by the imposition of a tax. For example, if the supply curve in the diagram had been perfectly elastic the tax revenue would have fallen from P2 CBA to P1 HG P3.

Thus indirect taxation as a revenue raising weapon is only likely to be successful on products which have an inelastic demand. The problem here is that it is mainly products such as foodstuffs which have inelastic demand curves, and these are the very products which governments do not wish to tax for very obvious reasons. This is why the very few relatively inelastic products which we have which are not essentials, such as petrol and cigarettes, are taxed so heavily. (What is essential is a matter of habit and taste.) Note that the 1974 March Labour budget expected to raise an extra £680 million from indirect taxation, most of it from petrol, cigarettes, beer and gambling duties. The tax yield was uncertain because of the possibility of a drop in sales.

5. British monopoly policy

Here, we intend to evaluate British monopoly policy in the light of two major objectives. The first is the extent to which it discouraged the formation of monopolistic market structures. The second is the extent to which it discouraged non-competitive behaviour within existing market structures, particularly with regard to pricing.

a) *The discouragement of monopolistic market structures*

When Britain's monopoly policy was initiated with the introduction of the Monopolies and Restrictive Practices Act in 1948, it was not clear that the objective was to foster competition. Indeed, the major function of the Monopolies Commission which was set up was to examine the extent of monopoly and to consider whether it was detrimental to economic efficiency. Thus the Commission was concerned not only with competition, but also with efficiency, and indeed with anything else which might be deemed relevant to the public interest. The Board of Trade had the power to request the Commission to investigate any trade where one-third of a class of goods was supplied in the U.K. by a firm or a group of firms acting together so as to restrict competition. The problem was that when the Commission investigated companies it considered information on all sorts of issues because it was uncertain what information would in the final analysis prove to be relevant. It is little wonder that in many cases the investigation of a company took a number of years. This tardy operation of the Commission which lengthy investigations led to, has considerably reduced its effectiveness.

Thus the initial premise of British monopoly policy was not that competition was good and monopoly was bad, but rather that it was necessary to investigate each case on its own merits. This was partly due to the arguments that monopolization leads to economies of scale and consequent cost and price reductions, and partly due to the more dynamic arguments that monopolistic market structures foster research and development. In the event, this piecemeal approach meant that British monopoly policy has been extremely permissive in so far as single firm monopolies are concerned. This tentative

145

approach towards single firm monopolies was reaffirmed in part 3 of the 1956 Restrictive Trade Practices Act.

It was not until the 1973 Fair Trading Bill that a more aggressive approach to monopoly policy was introduced in Britain. The objective is now no longer shackled by vague references to efficiency but is stated quite clearly as being 'the desirability . . . of maintaining and promoting effective competition'.[9] Thus the new approach is much less pragmatic than the 1948 legislation in that it recognizes the merits of competition as opposed to monopoly. Nevertheless, even the 1973 legislation is not entirely dogmatic in its condemnation of monopoly in that the Commission, renamed the Monopolies and Mergers Commission, can still take account of all issues relevant to the public interest. It remains to be seen whether competition will be regarded as the major issue relevant to the public interest. In this respect it is worth noting that the 1973 Bill considerably widened the criteria for monopoly reference to include a quarter market share, local monopolies and nationalized industries, and that the power to make monopoly references now rests with the Director-General of Fair Trading, who himself may be overruled by the Secretary of State.

In so far as merger activity is concerned the first domestic legislation to take place was the 1965 Monopolies and Mergers Act. This gave the Board of Trade the power to refer a merger or proposed merger to the Monopolies Commission whenever the merger would create or increase a monopoly position as defined by the 1948 Monopolies Act or whenever the value of the assets to be taken over exceeds £5 million. These dual terms of reference meant that not only horizontal mergers but also vertical and conglomerate mergers were embraced by the new legislation.

However, there has been considerable dissatisfaction with merger policy in Britain. In the first place the selection of mergers to be investigated by the Commission has been extremely haphazard largely because of the Board of Trade's view that 'it would not be appropriate in Britain to formulate precise guidelines to determine which mergers will be referred by the Board to the Commission'.[10] Thus business firms were uncertain as to whether their proposed mergers would be referred, and only a small number of references have in fact been made. In this respect the 1973 Fair Trading Bill did not improve matters in that references are now to be made by the Minister, with the result that they are more likely to be made on political grounds. A second major criticism of merger policy has been its permissive attitude towards horizontal mergers. Of 700 mergers between 1965 and 1972, 80 per cent were horizontal, 10 per cent vertical and 10 per cent conglomerate.[11] This permissive attitude may have been partly due to the fact that during this period the Industrial Reorganization Corporation came into being with the objective of promoting rationalization, mainly through mergers.

Thus monopoly and merger policy in Britain has so far not been particularly successful in discouraging the formation of monopolistic market structures. Monopoly policy itself has worked extremely slowly and in a piecemeal fashion whereas merger policy has been dogged with the uncertainty surrounding reference and has done little to discourage horizontal mergers, the types of mergers most likely to lead to monopoly power.

(b) *The discouragement of non-competitive behaviour*

The work of the Monopolies Commission after 1948 revealed a wealth of information concerning non-competitive behaviour within existing market structures. The Commission was highly critical of non-competitive behaviour such as quota schemes, price fixing between firms, exclusive dealing, etc. However, it was not until the 1956 Restrictive Trade Practices Act that the government used general legislation against such non-competitive behaviour. Part 1 of the 1956 Act required that all restrictive agreements (i.e. agreements on price, quantities to be produced, areas to be supplied, conditions of sale, etc.) be registered with the Registrar of the Restrictive Practices Court which was set up. All such restrictive agreements were now regarded as operating against the public interest, and in the event the Act proved successful in leading to the abandonment of the majority of restrictive agreements.

This does not however mean that the 1956 Act was successful in promoting competition, particularly price competition. In the first place there were seven escape routes provided for in the Act which companies could use to prove to the Court that their restrictive agreements were beneficial to the public interest and should therefore be allowed to continue. The escape routes required each restriction to satisfy one or more of the following criteria; it was necessary to protect the public against injury; it conferred specific and substantial benefits on the consuming public; it was necessary to counteract restrictive measures taken by a person outside the agreement; it was necessary to enable fair terms to be negotiated with a large supplier or purchaser; the removal of the restriction would cause serious and persistent unemployment; its removal would cause a reduction in exports; or that it was a necessary support to other restrictions in the agreement which are in the public interest. Moreover, there was an extra addition to these escape routes when in 1968 the Restrictive Trade Practices Act of that year allowed restrictions to be defended on the grounds that they do not restrict competition to any serious degree in any relevant trade or industry. Moreover, this Act also allowed registration to be avoided whenever the aim of the agreement was to promote efficiency or improve productive capacity. This weakening of the 1956 legislation was partly due to the growth of 'information agreements' whereby firms notified each other of issues such as prices and costs, and partly due to the inter-firm co-operation required by the work of the Economic Development Committees which were set up to stimulate exports and increase efficiency. Nevertheless, however admirable the objectives, the net effect of the 1968 legislation was to reduce control over non-competitive behaviour.

Moreover, the behaviour of those firms who abandoned their restrictive practices was not always perceptibly different from what it had been before. In some cases informal understandings and the experience of past behaviour were sufficient to bring about uniformity of behaviour between firms, particularly with regard to pricing. In other cases a system of price leadership developed, with smaller firms following the leadership of larger firms. In yet other cases, the abandonment of restrictive practices may have led to the development of mergers, so that indirectly part of the effect of restrictive practices legislation may have been to lead to the growth of more concentrated market structures.

Turning to the regulation of non-competitive behaviour within unitary monopolies, the emphasis on the whole has been on the development of more competitive pricing policies. Perhaps the best known cases of the Monopolies Commission investigating products sold on brand appeal rather than on price appeal have been the case of detergents in 1966[12] and breakfast cereals in 1973.[13] In the case of detergents its investigations led to the condemnation of excessive non-price competition in the form of advertising and brought about the introduction of fresh price competition. In the case of Kelloggs breakfast cereals the Commission recommended that the company's prices and profits be placed under continual government review so as to protect consumers against possible exploitation.

The government also found it necessary to stimulate price competition at the retail end of the market. Up until 1956 manufacturers had been able to maintain resale price either by individual or collective action, by restricting supplies to retailers who did not maintain the suggested price. It was under part 2 of the 1956 Restrictive Trades Practices Act that collective resale price maintenance was made illegal. However, it was not until the 1964 Resale Price Maintenance Act that individual resale price maintenance was made illegal. Once again there were to be escape routes through which firms could prove before the Court that the abandonment of resale price maintenance would be detrimental to the consumers in any of the following ways: that it would lead to a reduction in the quality or variety of the product; or a substantial reduction in the number of retail outlets; or a rise in retail prices; or a substantial reduction in necessary after sales service; or that the conditions under which the goods would be sold would be detrimental to the health of the consumers. Nevertheless, despite the existence of these escape routes there is no question that the 1964 Act was successful in achieving the abandonment of resale price maintenance. Many trades abandoned resale price maintenance as soon as the Act became law, while others finally succumbed with the decisions of the Restrictive Practices Court against the confectionery trade in 1967 and the footwear trade in 1968.

There can be no questioning the factt hat the abandonment

of resale price maintenance has led to price reductions on many goods. This can be observed in many shops today where the price charged is below the manufacturer's recommended retail price. There were, however, other effects of the 1964 Act. In the first place, it is important to note that the abandonment of resale price maintenance (along with the introduction of Selective Employment Tax) has led to an increased concentration in retailing, since the increased price competition has enabled the more efficient firms to expand their market share. Moreover, many of the retail organizations are now large enough to force favourable terms out of the manufacturers, and this has placed further pressure on the small retailers. Whether in the long run this increased concentration at the retail end will be beneficial in terms of the countervailing power they can use against manufacturers to wring favourable terms from them, or whether it will lead to reduced price competitiveness remains to be seen.

6 Conclusion

In the United Kingdom there is no question that government intervention in the price mechanism is here to stay. It is indeed ironic that the Conservative Party, traditionally the free enterprise party, is most adamant that statutory controls on prices and incomes must stay. In any case government intervention is essential for revenue raising and distributional reasons. Nevertheless, although necessary, government intervention in the price mechanism must be undertaken with extreme caution lest the distortion caused by intervention inhibits the response of demand and supply to the detriment of the entire resource allocation process.

REFERENCES

1. A. W. Phillips, 'The Relationship Between Unemployment and the Rate of Change of Money Wage Rates in the United Kingdom, 1861–1957', *Economica*, 1958.
2. H. Leibenstein, 'Allocative Efficiency Versus X-Efficiency', *A.E.R.*, June 1966.
3. 'The Uses of Prices and Incomes Policies in Britain', *Midland Bank Review*, August 1973.
4. D. Lee, *Control of the Economy*, Heinemann, 1974.

5. A. Cairncross, 'Incomes Policy; Retrospect and Prospect', *Three Banks Review*, December 1973.
6. J. Burton, *Wage Inflation*, Macmillan, 1972, Chapter 7.
7. R. G. Lipsey and J. M. Parkin, 'Incomes Policy; A Re-appraisal' *Economica*, 1970.
8. Cairncross, op. cit., p. 13.
9. Fair Trading Bill, 1973.
10. Board of Trade, *Mergers: A Guide to Board of Trade Practice*, H.M.S.O., 1969.
11. G. Bone, *British Economy Survey*, Spring 1973.
12. The Monopolies Commission, *Household Detergents: A Report on the Supply of Household Detergents*, H.M.S.O., 1966.
13. The Monopolies Commission, *Breakfast Cereals: A Report on the Supply of Ready-Cooked Breakfast Cereal Foods*, H.M.S.O., 1973.

PROGRESS TEST

1. Why would a government wish to stabilize the general level of prices? What means can it use to achieve this? (1a, 2a, b, c)
2. What is the Phillips curve? Does the analysis of the curve weaken or strengthen the case for a Prices and Incomes Policy? (1a, 2c)
3. What are the problems of attempting to fix individual prices above and below the equilibrium? Discuss in relation to subsidies, rationing and price support policies. (3a, 3b)
4. Under what conditions is indirect taxation likely to be successful as a revenue raising weapon? (4)
5. Assess the success of British monopoly policy in discouraging the formation of monopolistic market structures. (5a)
6. Evaluate the contribution of British monopoly policy to the stimulation of price competition in British industry. (5b)

INDEX